WILLIAM LECKIE MARTIN
"The Sheiling"
Bellevue Road
KIRKINTILLOCH

TWO MEN SEE LIFE

Printed in Great Britain

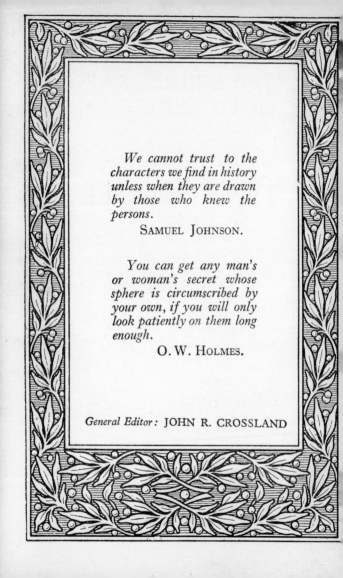

We cannot trust to the characters we find in history unless when they are drawn by those who knew the persons.

SAMUEL JOHNSON.

You can get any man's or woman's secret whose sphere is circumscribed by your own, if you will only look patiently on them long enough.

O. W. HOLMES.

General Editor : JOHN R. CROSSLAND

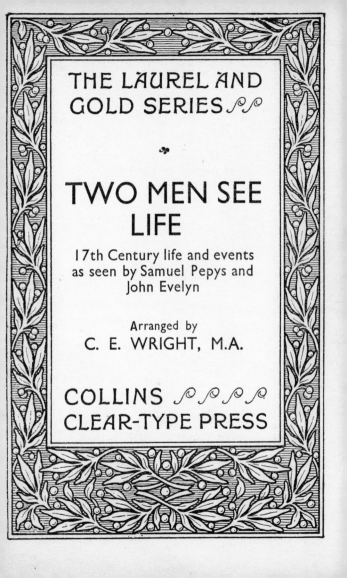

THE LAUREL AND GOLD SERIES

TWO MEN SEE LIFE

17th Century life and events
as seen by Samuel Pepys and
John Evelyn

Arranged by
C. E. WRIGHT, M.A.

COLLINS
CLEAR-TYPE PRESS

CONTENTS

INTRODUCTION

ENGLAND is fortunate in the possession of many good diarists. Two of the most famous, probably the most famous, were contemporaries and friends. These are Samuel Pepys and John Evelyn. Both wrote long and interesting works, but they are seldom read as books, partly because of the length, and partly because the stories they tell are so disconnected that following them is a difficult matter. But the stories are there and an attempt will be made to disentangle them and present them, in extracts, in an easier and, therefore, more attractive form.

The Times.

Had Pepys and Evelyn been offered the choice of any period of history to illustrate, they could not have selected a more stirring and appealing time than that in which they lived.

Foreign affairs centre round the splendid despotic figure of Louis XIV., King of France, whose rule, so greatly in contrast with that of England at that time, was the model for most countries of Europe. Both diarists have something to say about this monarch, but as this can be included in the story of political events in England, no attempt will be made to present foreign affairs as a separate story.

But our chief debt to the two diarists concerns

domestic affairs. These we may for convenience divide into five sections.

First comes the story of political events, a story unsurpassed in English History for importance and glamour. We start with the first two Stuarts, James I. (1603 to 1625) and Charles I. (1625 to 1649), who made a gallant effort to rule the land as despots. This only provoked a reaction, the Puritan Revolution (1640—1660), which set up the second two Stuarts, Charles II. (1660—1685) and James II. (1685—1688), as limited monarchs, despite the latter's wish to throw off his traces, an action which brought about a second and less important revolution, the Protestant Revolution of 1689. The political story could be carried on through the reign of William III. (1689—1702) and even into that of Anne.

To indicate the glamour of this period one need only mention such events as the Civil War, The Plague, The Fire, and such persons as Cromwell and his son (Tumble-Down-Dick), the Merry Monarch and his more serious brother, Lady Castlemaine and Nell Gwynn.

The second story in this record of domestic events we might justly call The Nation at Work. Up to this time England was a tool-using rather than a machine-using country: a land of agriculture rather than industry. The great events which were to work the change, the Industrial Revolution, were still somewhat distant. Hence we shall get a vastly different picture from the one England now presents. There were, however, signs that the change was coming. Industries were arising and our diarists do not omit them.

Our next subject for investigation will be the

Nation at its Studies. Learning in those days, both in schools and in universities differed greatly from modern education, and Pepys and Evelyn, representatives of Cambridge and Oxford respectively, tell us much about the system in their days. But perhaps even more interesting is their account of the intellectual progress in Stuart times revealed in a famous society which originated under Charles II., the Royal Society. There was, indeed, in later Stuart days, a second Renaissance.

Perhaps the fourth story, that of the social life of the times, will be the most interesting. If, as many claim, it be true that the record of the habits and pastimes of the people is as important as that of political events, then the diarists have laid us under a deep obligation, for there are few pages in the diaries which have not some account of the customs of the day. Especially is this true of the pleasure-loving Pepys, whose pages teem with accounts of weddings, christenings, musical parties and theatre visits. We might well term this section, The Nation at Play.

To wind up the tale it may be appropriate to see the nation in a more serious aspect, and follow the story of religion. Here again there is a record of progress from the time of the bigoted Puritans of Cromwell's day and that which expressed its hatred of all dissent in the Clarendon Code, to the days of William III. when toleration was established. Both Pepys and Evelyn were closely attached to the Church of England though their motives for Church attendance differed considerably. It is this difference of attitude which enriches the story they have to tell of the Nation at Worship.

The Diaries.

The diaries, in thus illustrating the above sections of our national life, will have covered a fairly comprehensive field. But it would be a mistake to imagine that the work they perform is identical. On the contrary they are complementary and our account would be not only much poorer but sadly incomplete if we were deprived of either. A glance at each will reveal its nature and the part it plays in History.

Although far longer than Evelyn's work, Pepys's diary covers a much shorter period. Commencing on January 1st, 1660, Pepys continued his record until failing eyesight compelled him to relinquish his task on May 31st, 1669, when he writes :

" And thus ends all that I doubt I shall ever be able to do with my own eyes in the keeping of my Journal, I being not able to do it any longer, having done now so long as to undo my eyes almost every time that I take a pen in my hand ; and, therefore, whatever comes of it, I must forbear : and, therefore, resolve, from this time forward, to have it kept by my people in long-hand, and must be contented to set down no more than is fit for them and all the world to know ; or, if there be any thing, I must endeavour to keep a margin in my book open, to add, here and there, a note in short-hand with my own hand.

" And so I betake myself to that course, which is almost as much as to see myself go into my grave : for which, and all the discomforts that will accompany my being blind, the good God prepare me ! "

This extract reveals something of the author's method of compiling his book. Writing in a way which suggests he was chatting to himself, Pepys took great care to preserve the diary from prying eyes. It was written in a form of shorthand, while still further to disguise the contents, he enters specially private matter, as one writer says, in a curious mixture of foreign languages. So eager was he to guard its secrecy that on July 2nd, 1662, he rose " while the chimes went four, and so put down my journal." Again on January 16th, 1660, he writes :

" I stayed up till the bell-man came by with his bell just under my window as I was writing of this very line, and cried, ' Past one of the clock, and a cold, frosty, windy morning.' ". To only one man did he reveal the existence of his diary and that was Sir William Coventry, Charles II.'s minister. On March 9th, 1669, he writes :

" Up, and to the Tower ; and there find Sir W. Coventry alone, writing down his Journal, which, he tells me, he now keeps of the material things ; upon which I told him, and he is the only man I ever told it to, I think, that I kept it most strictly these eight or ten years ; and I am sorry almost that I told it him, it not being necessary, nor may be convenient, to have it known."

Pepys has thus given us much of his personal experience, and has recorded most things that came his way. His curiosity was insatiable but he is not merely an annalist : he is more—he is a commentator. Many of his remarks on the social customs of the times, on the plays he witnessed, on the sermons he heard, are notable.

The great value of the diary is the light it sheds on social life. His accounts of political affairs, although he was in personal contact with people of high rank—the King and the Duke of York often spoke with him—frequently appear second-hand. His custom is to report what some one tells him and his avidity for news often leads him to accept facts, the improbability of which would strike an ordinary listener. Witness the false account of Louis XIV. which Pepys obtains on June 28th, 1667:

"At table, my Lady and Sir Philip Carteret have great and good discourse of the greatness of the present King of France—what great things he hath done, that a man may pass, at any hour of the night, all over that wild city [Paris], with a purse in his hand and no danger : that there is not a beggar to be seen in it, nor dirt lying in it ; that he hath married two of Colbert's daughters to two of the greatest princes of France, and given them portions—bought the greatest dukedom in France, and given it to Colbert ; and ne'er a prince in France dare whisper against it, whereas here our King cannot do any such thing, but everybody's mouth is open against him for it, and the man that hath the favour also. That to several commanders that had not money to set them out to the present campagne, he did of his own accord send them £1000 sterling a-piece, to equip themselves. But then they did enlarge upon the slavery of the people—that they are taxed more than the real estates they have ; nay, it is an ordinary thing for people to desire to give the King all their land that they have, and themselves become only his tenants, and pay him rent for the full value for it : so they may have but their earnings. But this will not be granted ; but he shall give the value of his rent, and part of his labour too. That there is not a petty governor of a province—

nay, of a town, but he will take the daughter from the richest man in the town under him, that hath got anything, and give her to his footman for a wife if he pleases, and the King of France will do the like to the best man in his kingdom—take his daughter from him, and give her to his footman, or whom he pleases."

Pepys's accounts of the intellectual and religious life of the times are valuable, but he has little to say on economic matters. Most of the gaps left by Pepys are filled in by Evelyn, and thus the diaries are largely complementary. Although we should not think of going to Evelyn rather than to Pepys for our account of social life, yet Evelyn has much to say concerning the ways of our ancestors. But when political affairs are concerned, we have in Evelyn a shrewd and sane observer. The diary covers a much longer period than that of Pepys, for, commencing with personal records from his birth in 1620, he gradually enlarges the scope and entries of his book until towards the end of his life the entries become more scanty, his last year, 1705—1706, filling but one page.

It is this commenting on political affairs of which they were contemporaries which has led some to draw a contrast between Evelyn's work and that of Pepys and to style the former, not a diary but a *memoir*. It is certainly the more useful to us when studying political history, for not only does it cover the periods of Charles I., the Civil War and the later Stuarts, but it also speaks with a surer tone. An intimate friend of the King, Evelyn moved more easily than Pepys in the highest circles, and so his accounts read with more conviction. Other gaps which Evelyn fills are the

stories of intellectual and economic progress. As
secretary of the Royal Society and as a commissioner for farming he came into close contact
with phases of English life for the study of which
Pepys had not equal opportunity.

The Writers.

The divergences in the works of our two diarists
are largely due to the difference of their lives and
outlook, so that a brief account of the men is
imperative.

Samuel Pepys.

Pepys was essentially a Londoner, although his
family can be traced back to Cambridgeshire.
His father, John Pepys, was a younger son of a
middle-class family, and his lot was that of many
younger sons : he had to engage in trade, a proceeding which was then looked upon by the gentry
as a misfortune. John further strengthened his
connections with trade by his marriage. Of his
father, who was a tailor, Samuel speaks with
tenderness and respect, but he has little good to
report of his mother's family, the " Kites," who
were connected with the butchering trade. On
September 12th, 1661, he writes :

" To my aunt Kite's in the morning, to help
my uncle Fenner to put things in order against
anon for the burial. After sermon, with my wife
to the burial of my aunt Kite, where, besides us
and my uncle Fenner's family, there was none of
any quality, but poor and rascally people. So
we went to church with the corps, and there had
service read at the grave, and back again with
Pegg Kite, who will be, I doubt, a troublesome

carrion to us executors, but if she will not be ruled, I shall fling up my executorship.''

With the rest of his family Samuel had trouble, for as he grew richer he found the claims of his needy relatives more and more pressing. But he appears to have treated all generously. He even found a husband for his troublesome sister, Paulina. His relations with his wife, a pretty though poor daughter of a Huguenot refugee, were often strained, partly because of his devotion to beauty. Pepys records on September 6th, 1662 :

"Called upon Doll, our pretty 'Change woman, for a pair of gloves trimmed with yellow ribbon, to [match] the petticoat my wife bought yesterday, which cost me 20s. ; but she is so pretty, that, God forgive me ! I could not think it too much, which is a strange slavery that I stand in to beauty, that I value nothing near it.''

This devotion, however, had its dangers, and Pepys felt the need for protecting himself against its snares by a series of punitive fines. On Feb. 3rd, 1665, we read :

"To my uncle Wight's where the Wights all dined ; and, among the others, pretty Mrs. Margaret, who indeed is a very pretty lady ; and, though by my vow it costs me 12d. a kiss after the first, yet I did adventure upon a couple.''

These punishments were apparently not very effective for Mrs. Pepys's jealousy was frequently aroused and words did not always settle their quarrels. On January 12th, 1669, we read of Mrs. Pepys attacking her spouse with red hot tongs.

To his life Pepys makes many references. Born in London in 1633, he was educated partly at St.

Paul's School. Of his early days he proudly says on May 11th, 1667 :

"Walked over the fields to Kingsland, and back again ; a walk, I think, I have not taken these twenty years ; but puts me in mind of my boy's time, when I boarded at Kingsland, and used to shoot with my bow and arrows in these fields. A very pretty place it is ; and little did any of my friends think I should come to walk in these fields in this condition and state that I am."

Again on April 26th, 1664, he writes :

"Thence, the young ladies going out to visit, I took my wife by coach out through the city, discoursing how to spend the afternoon ; and conquered, with much ado, a desire of going to the play ; but took her out at White Chapel, and took her out to Bednal Green ; so to Hackney, where I have not been many a year, since a little child I boarded there. Thence to Kingsland by my nurse's house, Goody Lawrence, where my brother Tom and I was kept when young. Then to Newington Green, and saw the outside of Mrs. Herbert's house, where she lived, and my aunt Ellen with her ; but, Lord ! how in every point I find myself to over-value things when a child."

From St. Paul's he migrated to Cambridge where he graduated. While here he revealed characteristics for which he is noted later. On October 21st, 1653, he was censured for being "scandalously overseene in drink." That he knew his weaknesses is seen by the entry on December 31st, 1661, where he says :

"I have newly taken a solemn oath about abstaining from plays and wine, which I am resolved to keep, according to the letter of the oath which I keep by me."

But vows are often weak cords for binding a man, and Pepys sometimes found amusing methods of evading them. On the 29th October, 1663, we read the following concerning a visit to the Guildhall :

" We went into the Buttry, and there stayed and talked, and then into the Hall again, and there wine was offered, and they drunk, I only drinking some hypocras, which do not break my vowe, it being to the best of my present judgement, only a mixed compound drink, and not any wine. If I am mistaken, God forgive me ! but I hope and think I am not."

For Magdalen College he had a great love and it is there that we now find the magnificent collection of volumes that Pepys so assiduously amassed.

His official life reads like a romance. In 1660, a penniless dependent on his kinsman, Lord Sandwich, Pepys quickly proved his worth and was made one of the four Tellers of the Exchequer, and in the same year the Clerk of the Acts to the Navy Board which managed the civil side of the work of the navy. It is surprising to learn that at this time Pepys did not know even his multiplication tables, but he never allowed grass to grow under his feet. On July 4th, 1662, we read :

" Comes Mr. Cooper, mate of the *Royall Charles*, of whom I intend to learn mathematiques, and do begin with him to-day, he being a very able man, and no great matter, I suppose, will content him. After an houre's being with him at arithmetique, my first attempt being to learn the multiplication-table : then we parted till to-morrow."

On the 11th of the same month he writes :

" Up by four o'clock, and hard at my multipli-cacion-table, which I am now almost master of."

Next year we find Mrs. Pepys having to oblige her rather exacting husband by taking a similar course of training, for on December 6th the pair spent their Sabbath afternoon at arithmetic and the diarist notes with pride that his wife " is come to do Addition, Subtraction, and Multiplication very well."

Other offices soon came his way. In 1662 he was made a Younger Brother of Trinity House, a cor-poration which supervised our mercantile marine. In the same year he was appointed one of the com-missioners to whose hands was entrusted the regulation of our recently acquired possession, Tangiers. Two years later Pepys acted on a com-mission dealing with the fisheries. In 1665 he was elected Fellow of the Royal Society. And so the story continues.

Another illustration of this growing importance is to be seen in his increasing wealth. In 1660 he is worth £40 ; in 1662, £650 ; in 1665, £1900 ; while the close of 1666 sees him with over £6000. This wealth became a care owing to the absence of reliable bankers and thus during the Dutch War in 1667 Pepys sent his wife to his father's estate at Brampton, near Huntingdon, to bury it. When later Pepys came to resurrect his gold there is a scene such as Pepys alone can tell. After having discovered the hidden gold they found :

" that the bags were all rotten, and all the notes, that I could not tell what in the world to say to it, not knowing how to judge what was wanting, or what had been lost by Gibson in his coming down :

which, all put together, did make me mad; and at last I was forced to take up the head-pieces, dirt and all, and as many of the scattered pieces as I could with the dirt discern by candle-light, and carry them up into my brother's chamber, and there locke them up till I had eat a little supper: and then, all people going to bed, W. Hewer and I did all alone, with several pails of water and besoms, at last wash the dirt off of the pieces, and parted the pieces and the dirt, and then began to tell them by a note which I had of the value of the whole, in my pocket; and do find that there was short above a hundred pieces: which did make me mad; and considering that the neighbour's house was so near that we could not possibly speak one to another in the garden at that place where the gold lay—especially my father being deaf—but they must know what we had been doing, I feared that they might in the night come and gather some pieces and prevent us the next morning; so W. Hewer and I out again about midnight, for it was now grown so late, and there by candle-light did make shift to gather forty-five pieces more. And so in, and to cleanse them: and by this time it was past two in the morning; and so to bed, with my mind pretty quiet to think that I have recovered so many."

It is sad to see any one in declining fortune, a lot that befel Pepys during one stage of his career. For a time he was actually in prison where he was visited by Evelyn, who says, on June 4th, 1679:

" I dined with Mr. Pepys in the Tower, he having been committed by the House of Commons for misdemeanors in the Admiralty when he was Secretary; I believe he was unjustly charged."

On the other hand, later, in 1684, Pepys had the gratification of being elected President of the Royal Society, a position he held for two years. Among the Fellows whom he entertained on Saturday evenings, probably none was more honoured than his fellow diarist, Evelyn, who in his turn had a high respect for Pepys, for he describes him as "extraordinary, ingenious and knowing." The death of Pepys on May 26th, 1703, drew forth the following panegyric in Evelyn's Diary:

"This day died Mr. Samuel Pepys, a very worthy, industrious and curious person, none in England exceeding him in knowledge of the navy, in which he had passed through all the most considerable offices, Clerk of the Acts and Secretary of the Admiralty, all which he performed with great integrity. When King James II. went out of England, he laid down his office, and would serve no more; but withdrawing himself from all public affairs, he lived at Clapham with his partner, Mr. Hewer, formerly his clerk, in a very noble house and sweet place, where he enjoyed the fruit of his labours in great prosperity. He was universally beloved, hospitable, generous, learned in many things, skilled in music, a very great cherisher of learned men of whom he had the conversation. His library and collection of other curiosities were of the most considerable, the models of ships especially. Besides what he published of an account of the navy, as he found and left it, he had for divers years under his hand the History of the Navy, or *Navalia*, as he called it; but how far advanced, and what will follow of his, is left, I suppose, to his sister's son, Mr. Jackson, a young gentleman,

whom Mr. Pepys had educated in all sorts of useful
learning, sending him to travel abroad, from whence
he returned with extraordinary accomplishments,
and worthy to be heir. Mr. Pepys had been for
near forty years so much my particular friend, that
Mr. Jackson sent me complete mourning, desiring
me to be one to hold up the pall at his magnificent
obsequies; but my indisposition hindered me
from doing him this last office."

John Evelyn.

Turning to Evelyn we come to a man who though
a great contrast to the pleasure loving, credulous
and garrulous Pepys, had yet this in common with
him—he was an earnest searcher for knowledge.
The opening pages of his Diary give an account
of his early life. Born in 1620 at Wotton or Black-
heath, Surrey, he from the commencement moved
in high society. Nevertheless he was denied the
privilege of education at any well-known school.
He was first taught in the church porch at Wotton,
and then received private tuition in Latin. His
father's fear of the severe discipline at Eton kept
John from that school, and so he was consigned
to the free school at Southover until sent to
the University. It was in 1637 that he entered
Balliol College, Oxford, then under the régime
of Chancellor Laud. His outlook on life might
reasonably be expected to differ somewhat from
that of the Cambridge-bred Pepys. Evelyn devel-
oped into the best type of Cavalier, one who loved
his King and his Church; but although a soldier—
he had " trailed a pike " in 1641—he is not found
fighting for his King during the Civil War. Charles I.
gave him a special dispensation to travel and much

of his time from 1641 to the Restoration was spent
abroad. Here he gains a wider experience than
Pepys. It was in 1647, while on his tours, that he
married the daughter of Charles II.'s ambassador
in Paris. During the Puritan Revolution Evelyn
was undisturbed, though the direction of his
sympathies was always with the King, whose
restoration he tried to bring about. Under the
date December 10th, 1659, he writes :

"I treated privately with Colonel Morley, then
Lieutenant of the Tower, and in great trust and
power, concerning delivering it to the King, and
the bringing of him in, to the great hazard of my
life, but the Colonel had been my school-fellow,
and I knew would not betray me."

With this constant loyalty it is interesting to
contrast the attitude of Pepys revealed when
dining with an old school-fellow on November 1st,
following the Restoration. Pepys was very apprehensive, for his friend "did remember that I was
a great Roundhead when I was a boy, and I was
much afraid that he would have remembered the
words that I said the day the King was beheaded
(that, were I to preach upon him, my text should
be—'The memory of the wicked shall rot ')."

With the Restoration, Evelyn's more active
political life commences. On March 31st, 1661,
he notes : "This night, his Majesty promised to
make my Wife Lady of the Jewels (a very honourable charge) to the future Queen (but which he
never performed)."

On the 19th of the following month honour came
to our diarist, but with modesty he refused.
Can we imagine Pepys doing the same ? Evelyn
writes : "To London, and saw the bath-ing and

rest of the ceremonies of the Knights of the Bath, preparatory to the coronation ; it was in the Painted Chamber, Westminster. I might have received this honour ; but declined it."

He did not, however, put aside the work that came his way. In 1662 he was chosen one of the commissioners " for reforming the buildings, ways, streets and encumbrances, and regulating the hackney coaches in the City of London." The same year saw him on a commission " to inquire how the City had disposed of the revenues of Gresham College." Two years later he was helping to regulate the Mint, while when the Dutch War broke out in this same year he was one of the commissioners to whose care the sick, wounded and prisoners were entrusted. Unlike Pepys, whose chief interests were in the town, Evelyn was always attracted to the country, and thus there is little wonder that in 1666 he was called upon to investigate the state of farming. To this duty was joined another—that of investigating the production of saltpetre : no more fitting person could have been chosen than the representative of a house engaged in its manufacture. It was in the same year that Evelyn served on a commission for the repair of St. Paul's. Reference has been made to his work on the Commission for Plantations. Again in 1695 his services were required, this time to sit on a commission exercising the duties of the Lord Privy Seal while that official was in Ireland. Ten years after this, Evelyn was on another commission —that " for endowing an Hospital for Seamen at Greenwich." What an amazingly varied list of activities !

It speaks much for Evelyn's versatility that he

was required for so many different tasks, and that
he performed his work well, there is little doubt.
In this thoroughness he is at one with Pepys.
Yet, despite their friendship and their occasional
resemblances, the note that must strike one on
reading the diaries is that of the abiding differences
between the high-souled, serene and scholarly
cavalier, and the roguish, irascible Clerk of the Acts
who was still generous enough to say of his friend,
" I find him a very fine gentleman." It is seldom
that Pepys pays a tribute unless it is specially
merited and so we can rely that these concluding
testimonials were warranted. On November 5th,
1665, Pepys says that Evelyn was " a man so much
above others," and, later, that one of his trans-
lations is " above my reach." On February 20th,
1666, Pepys finds him " a most excellent humoured
man . . . and mighty knowing." That Evelyn
was no gloomy Puritan is evident from Pepys's
entry on September 10th, 1665, concerning a supper
at which both were present :

" Among other humours, Mr. Evelyn's repeating
of some verses made up of nothing but the various
acceptations of *may* and *can*, and doing it so aptly
upon occasion of something of that nature, and so
fast, did make us all die almost with laughing, and
did so stop the mouth of Sir J. Minnes in the middle
of all his mirth, and in a thing agreeing with his
own manner of genius, that I never saw any man
so out-done in all my life ; and Sir J. Minnes's
mirth, too, to see himself out-done, was the crown
of all our mirth."

CHAPTER I

THE POLITICAL STORY

The Story up to 1649 : *Home affairs.*

IN the early part of his Diary Evelyn gives a few references to the struggle between King and Parliament which ended so unhappily for monarchy; but these initial entries are occasionally warped by the writer's unbounded loyalty to his monarch. One cause of their differences was foreign affairs, which were badly managed by the King. Charles I.'s favourite, Buckingham, was about to lead an ill-advised expedition against the French in 1628 when he was murdered. Evelyn says : " I very well remember that general muster previous to the Isle of Rhè's expedition, and that I was one day awakened in the morning with the news of the Duke of Buckingham being slain by that wretch, Felton, after our disgrace before La Rochelle."

Another point in dispute between King and Parliament was the levy of Ship Money to which Parliament objected. Loyal Evelyn's comment is shrewd :

" On the 19th July, we made a short excursion to Rochester, and having seen the cathedral, went to Chatham to see the *Royal Sovereign*, a glorious vessel of burden lately built there, being for defence and ornament, the richest that ever spread cloth before the wind. She carried an hundred brass cannon, and was 1200 tons ; a rare sailer, the work of the famous Phineas Pett, inventor of the frigate-fashion of building, to this day practised. But what is to be deplored as to this vessel is, that it cost his Majesty the affections of his subjects, perverted by the malcontent great ones, who took occasion to quarrel for his having raised a very slight tax for the building of this, and equipping the rest of the navy, without an act of Parliament ; though, by the suffrages of the major part of the Judges the King might legally do in times of imminent danger, of which his Majesty was best apprised. But this not satisfying a jealous party, it was condemned as unprecedential, and not justifiable as to the Royal prerogative ; and, accordingly, the Judges were removed out of their places, fined, and imprisoned."

A third bone of contention was religion. Charles I.'s attempt to enforce his religion, that of the Church of England, not only on his English but also on his Scottish subjects, caused trouble. It was in Scotland that the King's policy was first actively resisted, but the people of England knew that the Scots were fighting the battle for England as well. Of the year 1638 Evelyn gives a biased and misleading account : " This was the fatal year wherein the rebellious Scots opposed the King, upon the pretence of the introduction of some new ceremonies and the Book of Common Prayer, and madly began our confusions, and their own destruction, too, as it proved in event."

Charles's ill success in Scotland forced him to return to England to consult his Parliament, the Short Parliament of 1640, of which Evelyn says on April 11th, 1640, " I went to London to see the solemnity of His Majesty's riding through the city in state to the Short Parliament, which began on the 13th following,—a very glorious and magnificent sight, the King circled with his royal diadem and the affections of his people."

A second expedition against the Scots, again a failure, was necessary, and the King returned south once more, this time to meet a more famous parliament, the Long Parliament of 1640. Concerning this event Evelyn is again misleading, for he writes :

" I saw his Majesty (coming from his Northern Expedition) ride in pomp and a kind of ovation, with all the marks of a happy peace, restored to the affections of his people, being conducted through London with a most splendid cavalcade ; and, on the 3rd November following (a day never to be mentioned without a curse), to that long ungrateful, foolish, and fatal Parliament, the beginning of all our sorrows for twenty years after, and the period of the most happy monarch in the world."

This Parliament quickly got the upper hand and Charles's chief ministers were brought to justice. The most dangerous, Strafford, was tried first :

" 15th April. I repaired to London to hear and see the famous trial of the Earl of Strafford, Lord Deputy of Ireland, who, on the 22nd of March, had been summoned before both Houses of Parliament, and now appeared in Westminster-hall, which was prepared with scaffolds for the Lords and Commons, who, together with the King, Queen, Prince, and flower of the noblesse, were spectators and auditors of the greatest malice and the greatest innocency that ever met before so illustrous an assembly. It was Thomas Earl of Arundel and Surrey, Earl Marshal of England, who was made

High Steward upon this occasion ; and the sequel is too well-known to need any notice of the event."

He was quickly brought to the scaffold :

" On the 12th of May, I beheld on Tower-hill the fatal stroke which severed the wisest head in England from the shoulders of the Earl of Strafford, whose crime coming under the cognizance of no human law or statute, a new one was made, not to be a precedent, but his destruction. With what reluctancy the King signed the execution, he has sufficiently expressed ; to which he imputes his own unjust suffering—to such exorbitancy were things arrived."

Meanwhile riots were breaking out in England :

" London, and especially the Court, were at this period in frequent disorders, and great insolences were committed by the abused and too happy City : in particular, the Bishop of Canterbury's Palace at Lambeth was assaulted by a rude rabble from Southwark, my Lord Chamberlain imprisoned, and many scandalous libels and invectives scattered about the streets, to the reproach of Government, and the fermentation of our since distractions."

Evelyn has recorded the opening campaign in the Civil War when Essex failed to check Charles's march on London in 1642, and thus the Londoners had to march out to Brentford to save their city :

" To Chichester, and hence the next day to see the siege of Portsmouth ; for now was that bloody difference between the King and Parliament broken out, which ended in the fatal tragedy so many years after. It was on the day of its being rendered to Sir William Waller ; which gave me an opportunity of taking my leave of Colonel Goring, the governor, now embarking for France. This day was fought that signal battle at Edgehill."

At Brentford Evelyn was actually with the King:

" The 12th November was the battle of Brentford, surprisingly fought ; and to the great consternation of the City, had his Majesty (as it was believed he would) pursued his advantage. I came in with my horse and arms just at the retreat ; but was not permitted to stay longer than the 15th, by reason of the army marching to Gloucester ; which would have left both me and my brothers exposed to ruin, without any advantage to his Majesty."

After sending contributions to the King, who made Oxford his headquarters, Evelyn was granted a royal licence to travel abroad, and thus we lose his services as an annalist of the First Civil War. As compensation for this loss we have an interesting account of continental manners and customs.

In 1647 Evelyn was recalled to England on business, and so we get from him a few glimpses of that last despairing effort on behalf of the King, the Second Civil War, and also of the trial and execution of Charles.

" Came up the Essex petitioners for an agreement betwixt his Majesty and the rebels. The 16th, the Surrey men addressed the Parliament for the same ; of which some of them were slain and murdered by Cromwell's guards, in the New Palace Yard." (May 5th, 1648.) " . . . There was a rising now in Kent, my Lord of Norwich being at the head of them. Their first rendezvous was in Broome-field, next my house at Sayes Court, whence they went to Maidstone, and so to Colchester, where was that memorable siege." (May 30th.)

The Army were determined to bring the King to the scaffold, forestalling on December 13th, 1648, an attempt by Parliament to come to an understanding with him:

"The Parliament now sat up the whole night, and endeavoured to have concluded the Isle of Wight Treaty; but were surprised by the rebel army; the Members dispersed, and great confusion every where in expectation of what would be next."

On the 17th of the same month Evelyn "got privately into the council of the rebel army, at Whitehall, where I heard horrid villanies." A month later he witnesses a similar scene: "To London. I heard the rebel, Peters, incite the rebel powers met in the Painted Chamber, to destroy his Majesty; and saw that archtraitor, Bradshaw, who not long after condemned him."

Of the scene on January 29th he is almost too horror-struck to speak:

"The villany of the rebels proceeding now so far as to try, condemn, and murder our excellent King on the 30th of this month, struck me with such horror, that I kept the day of his martyrdom a fast, and would not be present at that execrable wickedness; receiving the sad account of it from my brother George, and Mr. Owen, who came to visit me this afternoon, and recounted all the circumstances."

Affairs abroad.

In escaping the Civil War in England, Evelyn came to be a witness of a much greater and more terrible war, for the Thirty Years' War was raging in Europe between 1618 and 1648. This was an attempt on the part of the Roman Catholics to check the increasing power of the Protestants, and also an attempt by the rulers of Austria, aided by their relatives in Spain, to make themselves powerful in Germany.

Evelyn took an active part in the Thirty Years' War, about as important as his participation in the English Civil War. Coming in August, 1641, to Genep, a castle which had just fallen, he was out of courtesy enrolled in a company there. Here he performed some trifling duties :

" The 3rd August, at night, we rode about the lines of circumvallation, the general being then in the field. The next day, I was accommodated with a very spacious and commodious tent for my lodging ; as before I was with a horse, which I had at command, and a hut which during the excessive heats was a great convenience ; for the sun piercing the canvass of the tent, it was during the day unsufferable, and at night not seldom infested with mists and fogs, which ascended from the river.

6th August. As the turn came about, we were ordered to watch on a horn-work near our quarters, and trail a pike, being the next morning relieved by a company of French. This was our continual duty till the castle was re-fortified, and all danger of quitting that station secured ; whence I went to see a Convent of Franciscan Friars, not far from our quarters, where we found both the chapel and refectory full, crowded with the goods of such poor people as at the approach of the army had fled with them thither for sanctuary. On the day following, I went to view all the trenches, approaches, and mines, &c., of the besiegers ; and, in particular, I took special notice of the wheel-bridge, which engine his Excellency had made to run over the moat when they stormed the castle; as it is since described (with all the other particulars of this siege) by the author of that incomparable work, 'Hollandia Illustrata.' The walls and ramparts of earth, which a mine had broken and crumbled, were of prodigious thickness."

Passes were needed for travelling and one was never sure of one's reception. Contrast the following two episodes:

(1) "The next morning, I embarked for Lillo, having refused a convoy of horse which was offered me. The tide being against us, we landed short of the fort on the beach, where we marched half leg deep in mud, ere we could gain the dyke, which, being five or six miles from Lillo, we were forced to walk on foot very wet and discomposed; and then entering a boat we passed the ferry, and came to the castle. Being taken before the Governor, he demanded my pass, to which he set his hand, and asked two rix-dollars for a fee, which methought appeared very exorbitant in a soldier of his quality. I told him that I had already purchased my pass of the commissaries at Rotterdam; at which, in a great fury, snatching the paper out of my hand, he flung it scornfully under the table, and bade me try whether I could get to Antwerp without his permission: but I had no sooner given him the dollars, than he returned the passport surlily enough, and made me pay fourteen Dutch shillings to the cantone, or searcher, for my contempt, which I was glad to do for fear of further trouble, should he have discovered my Spanish pass, in which the States were therein treated by the name of rebels. Besides all these exactions, I

gave the commissary six shillings, to the soldiers
something, and, ere perfectly clear of this frontier,
thirty-one stivers to the man-of-war, who lay
blocking up the river betwixt Lillo and the opposite
sconce called Lifkinshoeck."

(2) "We sailed by several Spanish forts, out of
one of which, St. Mary's port, came a Don on board
us, to whom I showed my Spanish pass, which he
signed, and civilly dismissed us. Hence, sailing by
another man-of-war, to which we lowered our
topsails, we at length arrived at Antwerp."

From 1649 to the Restoration : Home affairs.

Evelyn's entries with reference to Commonwealth
and Protectorate days are few and reveal his
hostility to the republicans. He dismisses the
setting up of the republic in 1649 in few words:
"30th May. Un-kingship was proclaimed, and his
Majesty's statues thrown down at St. Paul's
Portico, and the Exchange."

Evelyn, however, was not badly treated by
those in power, for he was allowed to go abroad :
"17th June. I got a pass from the rebel Bradshaw,
then in great power."

He exults at the deaths of any rebels. Of the
funeral of Dorislaus in 1649 he says : "This night
was buried with great pomp, Dorislaus, slain at the
Hague, the villain who managed the trial against
his sacred Majesty."

Cromwell was no favourite of our diarist for in
1657 he writes : "The Protector Oliver, now affecting kingship, is petitioned to take the title on him
by all his new-made sycophant lords, &c. ; but
dares not, for fear of the fanatics, not thoroughly
purged out of his rebel army.

Of his death in the next year we read: "*3rd September*. Died that arch-rebel, Oliver Cromwell, called Protector." The entry concerning his funeral in the next month deserves note: "*22nd*. Saw the superb funeral of the Protector. He was carried from Somerset-House in a velvet bed of state, drawn by six horses, housed with the same; the pall held by his new Lords; Oliver lying in effigy, in royal robes, and crowned with a crown, sceptre, and globe, like a king. The pendants and guidons were carried by the officers of the army; the Imperial banners, achievements, &c., by the heralds in their coats; a rich caparisoned horse, embroidered all over with gold; a knight of honour, armed cap-a-pié, and, after all, his guards, soldiers, and innumerable mourners. In this equipage, they proceeded to Westminster: but it was the joy-fullest funeral I ever saw; for there were none that cried but dogs, which the soldiers hooted away with a barbarous noise, drinking and taking tobacco in the streets as they went."

The following year sees reaction setting in:

"*25th April*, 1659. A wonderful and sudden change in the face of the public; the new Protector, Richard, slighted; several pretenders and parties strive for the government: all anarchy and confusion; Lord have mercy on us!"

October 11th, 1659, saw worse confusion: "The Army now turned out the Parliament. We had now no government in the nation; all in confusion; no magistrate either owned or pretended, but the soldiers, and they not agreed. God Almighty have mercy on, and settle us!"

But the man who was to cut this Gordian knot

and ensure the restoration of the Monarch was General Monk, Earl of Albemarle:

" *3rd February*. Kept the Fast. General Monk came now to London out of Scotland; but no man knew what he would do, or declare, yet he was met on his way by the gentlemen of all the counties which he passed, with petitions that he would recall the old long-interrupted Parliament, and settle the nation in some order, being at this time in most prodigious confusion, and under no government, everybody expecting what would be next, and what he would do.

." *10th*. Now were the gates of the city broken down by General Monk; which exceedingly exasperated the city, the soldiers marching up and down as triumphing over it, and all the old army of the fanatics put out of their posts, and sent out of town.

" *11th*. A signal day. Monk, perceiving how infamous and wretched a pack of knaves would have still usurped the supreme power, and having intelligence that they intended to take away his commission, repenting of what he had done to the city, and where he and his forces were quartered, marches to Whitehall, dissipates that nest of robbers, and convenes the old Parliament, the Rump Parliament (so called as retaining some few rotten members of the other) being dissolved; and for joy whereof were many thousands of rumps roasted publicly in the streets at the bonfires this night, with ringing of bells, and universal jubilee. This was the first good omen."

It is now that Pepys joins in the story and as he played a part in the actual bringing back of Charles II. he is very expansive on the subject.

The earnest wishes of the people for a restoration of monarchy were seen as early as March, 1660 :

" 16th. To Westminster Hall, where I heard how the Parliament had this day dissolved themselves, and did pass very cheerfully through the Hall, and the Speaker without his mace. The whole Hall was joyful thereat, as well as themselves, and now they begin to talk loud of the King. To-night I am told, that yesterday, about five o'clock in the afternoon, one came with a ladder to the Great Exchange, and wiped with a brush the inscription that was on King Charles, and that there was a great bonfire made in the Exchange, and people called out, ' God bless King Charles the Second ! ' "

To smooth the way for his restoration, Charles sent in May a declaration from Breda promising to act moderately. Pepys's patron, Edward Montagu, Lord Sandwich, acted promptly on receiving it, and so ensured the support of the fleet for Charles :

" 3d. This morning my Lord showed me the King's declaration and his letter to the two Generals to be communicated to the fleet. The contents of the latter are his offer of grace to all that will come in within forty days, only excepting them that the Parliament shall hereafter except. That the sales of lands during these troubles, and all other things, shall be left to the Parliament, by which he will stand. The letter dated at Breda, April $\frac{4}{14}$, 1660, in the twelfth year of his reign. Upon the receipt of it this morning by an express, Mr. Phillips, one of the messengers of the Council from General Monk, my Lord summoned a council of war, and in the mean time did dictate to me how he would have the vote ordered which he would have pass this council. Which done, the Commanders all came on board, and the council sat in the coach (the first council of war that had been in my time), where I read the letter and declaration ; and while they were discoursing upon it, I seemed to draw up a vote, which, being offered, they passed. Not one man seemed to say No to it, though I am confident many in their hearts were against it. After this was done, I went up to the quarter-deck with my Lord and the Commanders, and there read both the papers and the vote ; which done, and demanding their opinion, the seamen did all of them cry out, ' God bless King Charles ! ' with the greatest joy imaginable."

Pepys made sure that his part in this proceeding should be remembered : " *4th.* I wrote this morning many letters, and to all the copies of the vote of the council of war I put my name, that if it should come in print my name may be to it. I sent a copy of the vote to Doling, inclosed in this letter :—

" ' Sir,—He that can fancy a fleet (like ours) in her pride, with pendants loose, guns roaring, caps flying, and the loud " Vive le Roys ! " echoed from one ship's company to another, he, and he only, can apprehend the joy this inclosed vote was received with, or the blessing he thought himself possessed of that bore it, and is—Your humble servant.' "

The decision of the fleet Sandwich sent privately to Charles : " About nine o'clock I got all my letters done, and sent them by the messenger that come yesterday. This morning come Captain Isham on board with a gentleman going to the King, by whom very cunningly, my Lord tells

me, he intends to send an account of this day's
and yesterday's actions here, notwithstanding he
had writ to the Parliament to have leave of them
to send the King the answer of the fleet. Since my
writing of the last paragraph, my Lord called me
to him, to read his letter to the King, to see whether
I could find any slips in it or no. And as much of
the letter as I can remember is thus :

" ' May it please your Most Excellent Majesty,'
and so begins.

" That he yesterday received from General Monk
his Majesty's letter and direction ; and that General
Monk had desired him to write to the Parliament
to have leave to send the vote of the seamen
before he did send it to him, which he had done by
writing to both Speakers ; but for his private
satisfaction he had sent it thus privately, (and so
the copy of the proceedings yesterday was sent
him) and that this come by a gentleman that come
this day on board, intending to wait upon his
Majesty, that he is my Lord's countryman, and
one whose friends have suffered much on his
Majesty's behalf. That my Lords Pembroke and
Salisbury are put out of the House of Lords.
That my Lord is very joyful that other countries
do pay him the civility and respect due to him ;
and that he do much rejoice to see that the King
do receive none of their assistance (or some such
words) from them, he having strength enough in
the love and loyalty of his own subjects to support
him. That his Majesty had chosen the best place,
Scheveling, for his embarking, and that there is
nothing in the world of which he is more ambitious
than to have the honour of attending his Majesty,
which he hoped would be speedy. That he had

commanded the vessel to attend at Helvetsluce till this gentleman returns, that so if his Majesty do not think it fit to command the fleet himself, yet that he may be there to receive his commands and bring them to his Lordship. He ends his letter, that he is confounded with the thoughts of the high expressions of love to him in the King's letter, and concludes,

" ' Your most loyall, dutifull, faithfull, and obedient subject and servant,—E. M.' ' "

Preparations were made in the fleet that was to fetch the King : " 13*th.* (Lord's day.) To the quarter-deck, at which the tailors and painters were at work, cutting out some pieces of yellow cloth in the fashion of a crown and C. R., and put it upon a fine sheet, and that into the flag instead of the State's arms, which after dinner was finished and set up."

The fleet then started for Holland and to judge by the next extract, Charles must have been found in a desperate condition : " This afternoon Mr. Edward Pickering told me in what a sad, poor condition for clothes and money the King was, and all his attendants, when he came to him first from my Lord, their clothes not being worth forty shillings the best of them. And how overjoyed the King was when Sir J. Greenville brought him some money ; so joyful, that he called the Princess Royal and Duke of York to look upon it, as it lay in the portmanteau, before it was taken out."

Pepys was one of the first to see the King : " At dinner in came Dr. Cade, a merry mad parson of the King's. And they two got the child and me (the others not being able to crowd in) to see the King, who kissed the child very affectionately. Then we kissed his, and the Duke of York's, and the Princess Royal's hands. The King seemed to be a very sober man ; and a very splendid Court he hath in the number of persons of quality that are about him, English, very rich in habit. From the King to the Lord Chancellor, who did lie bed-rid of the gout : he spoke very merrily to the child and me. After that, going to see the Queen of Bohemia, I met Dr. Fuller, whom I sent to a tavern with Mr. Edward Pickering, while I, and the rest went to see the Queen, who used us very respectfully : her hand we all kissed. She seems a very debonair, but a plain lady."

He had also the honour of helping to fire the first salute, a proceeding which almost proved disastrous to the diarist : " By the time we came on board again, news is sent us that the King is on shore ; so my Lord fired all his guns round twice, and all the fleet after him, which, in the end, fell into disorder, which seemed very handsome. The gun over against my cabin I fired myself to the King, which was the first time that he had been saluted by his own ships since this change ; but, holding my head too much over the gun, I had almost spoiled my right eye. Nothing in the world but giving of guns almost all this day."

On the 23rd the King embarked : " 23*d*. All the afternoon the King walked here and there, up and down, (quite contrary to what I thought him to have been) very active and stirring. Upon the quarter-deck he fell into discourse of his escape from Worcester, where it made me ready to weep to hear the stories that he told of his difficulties that he had passed through, as his travelling four days and three nights on foot, every step up to his

knees in dirt, with nothing but a green coat and
a pair of country breeches on, and a pair of country
shoes that made him so sore all over his feet, that
that he could scarce stir. Yet he was forced to
run away from a miller and other company, that
took them for rogues. His sitting at table at one
place, where the master of the house, that had not
seen him in eight years, did know him, but kept it
private ; when at the same table there was one,
that had been of his own regiment at Worcester,
could not know him, but made him drink the King's
health, and said that the King was at least four
fingers higher than he. At another place, he was
by some servants of the house made to drink,
that they might know that he was not a Roundhead,
which they swore he was. In another place, at his
inn, the master of the house, as the King was
standing with his hands upon the back of a chair by
the fireside, kneeled down and kissed his hand,
privately, saying, that he would not ask him who
he was, but bid God bless him whither he was
going. Then the difficulties in getting a boat to
get into France, where he was fain to plot with the
master thereof to keep his design from the foreman
and a boy, (which was all the ship's company) and
so get to Fécamp, in France. At Rouen he looked
so poorly, that the people went into the rooms before
he went away, to see whether he had not stole
something or other. In the evening, I went up to
my Lord, to write letters for England, which we
sent away with word of our coming, by Mr. Edward
Pickering. The King supped alone in the coach ;
after that I got a dish, and we four supped in my
cabin, as at noon. About bedtime, my Lord Bart-
lett (who I had offered my service to before) sent

for me to get him a bed, who with much ado I did get to bed to my Lord Middlesex, in the great cabin below, but I was cruelly troubled before I could dispose of him, and quit myself of him. So to my cabin again, where the company still was, and were talking more of the King's difficulties; as how he was fain to eat a piece of bread and cheese out of a poor body's pocket; how, at a Catholic house he was fain to lie in the priest's hole a good while in the house for his privacy. After that, our company broke up. We have all the Lords Commissioners on board us and many others. Under sail all night, and most glorious weather.

. . . . .

" 25*th*. By the morning we were come close to the land, and everybody made ready to get on shore. The King and the two Dukes did eat their breakfast before they went; and there being set some ship's diet before them, only to show them the manner of the ship's diet, they eat of nothing else but pease and pork, and boiled beef. I had Mr. Darcy in my cabin; and Dr. Clerke, who eat with me, told me how the King had given £50 to Mr. Shepley for my Lord's servants, and £500 among the officers and common men of the ship. I spoke to the Duke of York about business, who called me Pepys by name, and upon my desire did promise me his future favour. Great expectation of the King's making some Knights, but there was none. About noon (though the brigantine that Beale made was there ready to carry him) yet he would go in my Lord's barge with the two Dukes. Our Captain steered, and my Lord went along bare with him. I went, and Mr. Mansell, and one of the king's footmen, and a dog that the King loved, in a boat by ourselves, and so got on shore when the King did, who was received by General Monk with all imaginable love and respect at his entrance upon the land at Dover. Infinite the crowd of people and the gallantry of the horsemen, citizens, and noblemen of all sorts. The Mayor of the town come and give him his white staff, the badge of his place, which the King did give him again. The Mayor also presented him from the town a very rich Bible, which he took, and said it was the thing that he loved above all things in the world. A canopy was provided for him to stand under, which he did, and talked awhile with General Monk and others, and so into a stately coach there set for him, and so away through the town towards Canterbury, without making any stay at Dover. The shouting and joy expressed by all is past imagination. Seeing that my Lord did not stir out of his barge, I got into a boat, and so into his barge, and we back to the ship, seeing a man almost drowned that fell into the sea. My Lord almost transported with joy that he had done all this without any the least blur or obstruction in the world, that could give offence to any, and with the great honour he thought it would be to him. Being overtook by the brigantine, my Lord and we went out of our barge into it, and so went on board with Sir W. Batten and the Vice and Rear-Admirals. At night, I supped with the Captain, who told me what the King had given us. My Lord returned late, and at his coming did give me order to cause the mark to be gilded, and a Crown and C. R. to to be made at the head of the coach table, where the King to-day with his own hand did mark his height, which accordingly I caused the painter so to do, and is now done, as is to be seen."

For the part he had played in bringing back the King, Sandwich received his reward: "*27th.* (Lord's day.) Called up by John Goods to see the Garter and Heralds' coat, which lay in the coach, brought by Sir Edward Walker, King at Arms, this morning, for my Lord. My Lord had summoned all the Commanders on board him, to see the ceremony, which was thus: Sir Edward, putting on his coat, and having laid the George and Garter, and the King's letter to my Lord, upon a crimson cushion, (in the coach, all the Commanders standing by) makes three congees to him, holding the cushion in his arms. Then, laying it down with the things upon it upon a chair, he takes the letter, and delivers it to my Lord, which my Lord breaks open and gives him to read. It was directed to our trusty and well beloved Sir Edward Montagu, Knight, one of our Generals at sea, and our Companion elect of our Noble Order of the Garter. The contents of the letter are to show that the Kings of England have for many years made use of this honour, as a special mark of favour, to persons of good extraction and valour, and that many Emperors, Kings, and Princes of other countries have borne this honour; and that whereas my Lord is of a noble family, and hath now done the King such service by sea, at this time, as he hath done; he do send him this George and Garter to wear as Knight of the Order, with a dispensation for the other ceremonies of the habit of the Order, and other things, till hereafter, when it can be done."

Evelyn then takes up the story of the King's

reception in London : " *29th*. This day, his Majesty, Charles the Second came to London, after a sad and long exile and calamitous suffering both of the King and Church, being seventeen years. This was also his birth-day, and with a triumph of above 20,000 horse and foot, brandishing their swords, and shouting with inexpressible joy ; the ways strewed with flowers, the bells ringing, the streets hung with tapestry, fountains running with wine : the Mayor, Aldermen, and all the Companies, in their liveries, chains of gold, and banners ; Lords and Nobles, clad in cloth of silver, gold, and velvet ; the windows and balconies, all set with ladies ; trumpets, music, and myriads of people flocking, even so far as from Rochester, so as they were seven hours in passing the city, even from two in the afternoon till nine at night.

" I stood in the Strand and behold it, and blessed God. And all this was done without one drop of blood shed, and by that very army which rebelled against him : but it was the Lord's doing, for such a restoration was never mentioned in any history, ancient or modern, since the return of the Jews from their Babylonish captivity ; nor so joyful a day and so bright ever seen in this nation, this happening when to expect or effect it was past all human policy.

" *4th June*. I received letters of Sir Richard Browne's landing at Dover, and also letters from the Queen, which I was to deliver at Whitehall, not as yet presenting myself to his Majesty, by reason of the infinite concourse of people. The eagerness of men, women, and children, to see his Majesty, and kiss his hands, was so great, that he had scarce leisure to eat for some days, coming

as they did from all parts of the nation ; and the
King being as willing to give them that satisfaction,
would have none kept out, but gave free access to
all sorts of people."

Affairs abroad.

Foreign affairs during this period did not attract
Evelyn. It was the time when France was passing
through the troubles of the Civil War known as the
Fronde ; after which the strong monarchy is built
up. For seventy-two years (1643—1715) Louis
XIV. ruled France and the splendour of his person
and rule appealed to most men of the day. Evelyn
has given us a typical picture of Louis taking up
the reins of government in 1651 :

" *7th September*. I went to visit Mr. Hobbes, the
famous philosopher of Malmesbury, with whom I
had long acquaintance. From his window, we saw
the whole equipage and glorious cavalcade of the
young French Monarch, Louis XIV., passing to
Parliament, when first he took the kingly government on him, now being in his 14th year, out of
his minority and the Queen Regent's pupillage.
First, came the captain of the King's Aids, at
the head of 50 richly liveried ; next, the Queen-
Mother's light Horse, 100, the lieutenant being
all over covered with embroidery and ribbons,
having before him four trumpets habited in black
velvet, full of lace, and casques of the same. Then,
the King's Light Horse, 200, richly habited, with
four trumpets in blue velvet embroidered with gold,
before whom rid the Count d'Olonne coronet
[cornet], whose belt was set with pearl. Next went
the grand Prévôt's company on foot, with the
Prévôt on horseback ; after them, the Swiss in

black velvet toques, led by two gallant cavaliers habited in scarlet-coloured satin, after their country fashion, which is very fantastic ; he had in his cap a *pennach* of heron, with a band of diamonds, and about him twelve little Swiss boys, with halberds. Then, came the *Aide des Cérémonies ;* next, the grandees of court, governors of places, and lieutenants-general of provinces, magnificently habited and mounted ; among whom I must not forget the Chevalier Paul, famous for many sea-fights and signal exploits there, because it is said he had never been an Academist, and yet governed a very unruly horse, and besides his rich suit his Malta Cross was esteemed at 10,000 crowns. These were headed by two trumpets, and the whole troop, covered with gold, jewels, and rich caparisons, were followed by six trumpets in blue velvet also, preceding as many heralds in blue velvet *semée* with fleurs-de-lis, caduces in their hands, and velvet caps on their heads ; behind them, came one of the masters of the ceremonies ; then, divers marshals and many of the nobility, exceeding splendid ; behind them Count d' Harcourt, grand Ecuyer, alone, carrying the King's sword in a scarf, which he held up in a blue sheath studded with fleurs-de-lis ; his horse had for reins two scarfs of black taffata.

" Then, came abundance of footmen and pages of the King, new-liveried with white and red feathers; next, the *garde du corps* and other officers, and, lastly, appeared the King himself on an Isabella barb, on which a housing *semée*, with crosses of the Order of the Holy Ghost, and fleurs-de-lis ; the King himself, like a young Apollo, was in a suit so covered with rich embroidery, that one could perceive nothing of the stuff under it; he went almost the whole way with his hat in hand, saluting the ladies and acclamators, who had filled the windows with their beauty, and the air with *Vive le Roi.* He seemed a prince of a grave yet sweet countenance. After the King, followed divers great persons of the Court, exceeding splendid, also his esquires; masters of horse, on foot; then the company of *Exempts des Gardes,* and six guards of Scotch. Betwixt their files were divers princes of the blood, dukes, and lords; after all these, the Queen's guard of Swiss, pages, and footmen; then, the Queen-Mother herself, in a rich coach, with Monsieur the King's brother, the Duke of Orleans, and some other lords and ladies of honour. About the coach, marched her *Exempts des Gardes ;* then the company of the King's *Gens d'armes,* well mounted, 150, with four trumpets, and as many of the Queen's; lastly, an innumerable company of coaches full of ladies and gallants. In this equipage, passed the monarch to the Parliament, henceforth exercising his kingly government."

From the Restoration onwards.

Domestic and foreign affairs are so mingled in this period that no attempt will be made to keep the accounts apart.

The story so far as England is concerned, is that of a reaction against the strict Puritan days, resulting in loss of prestige for the Stuarts, who made a belated attempt to resume their power but only brought about their downfall in the Protestant Revolution of 1688.

Personnel.

It will be well first to glance at some of the

actors in this drama. Charles II. must be taken first. Of his appearance Pepys gives us an account in 1661 : " And while I am waiting there, in comes the King in a plain common riding-suit and velvet cap, in which he seemed a very ordinary man to one that had not known him."

On November 2nd, 1663, Pepys says : " I never till this day observed that the King is mighty gray." Neither was the diarist impressed by the King's public speaking : " Anon comes the King, and passed the Bill for repealing the Triennial Act, and another about Writs of Errour. I crowded in, and heard the King's speech to them ; but he speaks the worst that ever I heard man in my life : worse than if he read it all, and he had it in writing in his hand."

His lack of dignity shocked Pepys : " With Sir H. Cholmly to Westminster ; who by the way told me how merry the King and Duke of York and Court were the other day, when they were abroad a-hunting. They came to Sir G. Carteret's house at Cranbourne, and there were entertained, and all made drunk ; and being all drunk, Armerer did come to the King, and swore to him ' by God, Sir,' says he, ' you are not so kind to the Duke of York of late as you used to be.'—' Not I ? ' says the King. ' Why so ? '—' Why,' says he, ' if you are, let us drink his health.'—' Why, let us,' says the King. Then he fell on his knees and drank it ; and having done, the King began to drink it. ' Nay, Sir,' says Armerer, ' by God you must do it on your knees !' So he did, and then all the company : and having done it, all fell a-crying for joy, being all maudlin and kissing one another, the King the Duke of York, and the Duke of York the King :

and in such a maudlin pickle as never people were : and so passed the day. But Sir H.Cholmly tells me, that the King hath this good luck, that the next day he hates to have any body mention what he had done the day before, nor will suffer any body to gain upon him that way ; which is a good quality."

His indifference and laziness were marked : " This day, at White Hall, I overheard Sir W. Coventry propose to the King his ordering of some particular thing in the Wardrobe, which was of no great value ; but yet, as much as it was, it was of profit to the King and saving to his purse. The King answered to it with great indifferency, as a thing that it was no great matter whether it was done or no. Sir W. Coventry answered : ' I see your Majesty do not remember the old English proverb, " He that will not stoop for a pin, will never be worth a pound." ' And so they parted, the King bidding him do as he would ; which, methought, was an answer not like a King that did intend ever to do well." [Pepys, *January 2nd*, 1668.]

Little wonder that foreign governments began to have a poor opinion of such a King !

" To-day, for certain, I am told how in Holland publickly they have pictured our King with re-reproach : one way, is with his pockets turned the wrong side outward, hanging out empty ; another, with two courtiers, picking of his pockets ; and a third, leading of two ladies, while others abuse him ; which amounts to great contempt." [Pepys, *November 28th*, 1662.]

Yet this merry monarch, who discovered a pleasant way of walking called sauntering, had his good points. He had amazing energy : " Hence to

Graye's-Inn Walks, and there staid a good while ;
where I met with Ned Pickering, who told me what
a great match of hunting of a stag the King had
yesterday ; and how the King tired all their horses,
and come home with not above two or three able
to keep pace with him." [Pepys, *August 11th*, 1661.]

He is said to have dragged his courtiers out of
bed at early hours to play tennis, and that he played
vigorously is evident from the following entry by
Pepys on September 2nd, 1667 :

" From him I went to see a great match at tennis,
between Prince Rupert and one Captain Cooke
against Bab. May and the elder Chichly ; where
the King was, and Court ; and it seems they are
the best players at tennis in the nation. But this
puts me in mind of what I observed in the morning,
that the King, playing at tennis, had a steele-yard
carried to him ; and I was told it was to weigh him
after he had done playing ; and at noon Mr. Ashburnham told me that it is only the King's curiosity,
which he usually hath of weighing himself before
and after his play, to see how much he loses in
weight by playing : and this day he lost 4½lbs."

He was easy to approach as both diarists found :
" Thence to White Hall ; where the King, seeing
me, did come to me, and, calling me by name, did
discourse with me about the ships in the River :
and this is the first time that ever I knew the King
did know me personally ; so that hereafter I must
not go thither, but with expectation to be questioned, and to be ready to give good answers."
[Pepys, *April 17th*, 1665.]

" *30th April*, 1663. Came his Majesty to honour
my poor villa with his presence, viewing the gardens
and even every room of the house, and was pleased

to take a small refreshment. There were with him the Duke of Richmond, Earl of St. Alban's, Lord Lauderdale, and several persons of quality. [Evelyn.]

Others found that not only was he easy to approach but that it was profitable to approach him: " His Majesty began first to *touch for the evil !* according to custom, thus : his Majesty sitting under his state in the Banqueting-house, the chirurgeons cause the sick to be brought, or led, up to the throne, where they kneeling, the king strokes their faces, or cheeks with both his hands at once, at which instant a chaplain in his formalities says, " He put his hands upon them, and he healed them." This is said to every one in particular. When they have been all touched, they come up again in the same order, and the other chaplain kneeling, and having angel gold strung on white ribbon on his arm, delivers them one by one to his Majesty, who puts them about the necks of the touched as they pass, whilst the first chaplain repeats, " That is the true light who came into the world." Then follows, an epistle (as at first a Gospel) with the Liturgy, prayers for the sick, with some alteration ; lastly the blessing ; and then the Lord Chamberlain and the Comptroller of the Household bring a basin, ewer and towel, for his Majesty to wash." [Evelyn, *July 6th*, 1660.]

Of the King's mother and his two sisters Pepys has an interesting note on November 22nd, 1660 : " Mr. Fox came in presently, and did receive us with a great deal of respect ; and then did take my wife and I to the Queen's presence-chamber, where he got my wife placed behind the Queen's chaire, and the two Princesses come to dinner.

The Queen, a very little, plain old woman, and nothing more in her presence in any respect nor garbe than any ordinary woman. The Princesse of Orange I had often seen before. The Princesse Henrietta is very pretty, but much below my expectation ; and her dressing of herself with her haire frized short up to her eares did make her seem so much the less to me. But my wife standing near her with two or three black patches on, and well dressed, did seem to me much handsomer than she."

Of the Duke of York, the King's brother, Pepys was well qualified to speak, as he was associated with him in matters connected with the Navy. On April 1st, 1661, Pepys sees the Duke playing " pelemele " and on December 15th, 1662, admired his powers as a skater : " To the Duke, and followed him into the Park, where though the ice was broken and dangerous, yet he would go slide upon his scates, which I did not like, but he slides very well."

He was less impressed on the 18th of the same month on which date he wrote : " We went up and saw the Duke dress himself, and in his night habitt he is a very plain man."

Fond of hunting and of most other forms of sport, he never, like his brother, allowed his pleasures to interfere too seriously with his duties. On June 1st, 1664, Pepys pays him this compliment : " He tells me, above all, of the Duke of York, that he is more himself and more of judgment is at hand in him, in the middle of a desperate service, than at other times, as appeared in the business of Dunkirke, wherein no man ever did braver things, or was in hotter service in the close of that day, being surrounded with enemies ; and then, contrary to the advice of all about him, his counsel carried himself and the rest through them safe, by advising that he might make his passage with but a dozen with him ; ' For,' says he, ' the enemy cannot move after me so fast with a great body, and with a small one we shall be enough to deal with them : ' and, though he is a man naturally martiall to the hottest degree, yet a man that never in his life talks one word of himself or service of his own, but only that he saw such or such a thing, and lays it down for a maxime that a Hector can have no courage."

Of the arrival in May, 1662, of that pathetic figure, Queen Catherine, Evelyn gives an interesting account :

" 25th. I went this evening to London, in order to our journey to Hampton Court, to see the new Queen, who, having landed at Portsmouth, had been married to the King a week before by the Bishop of London.

" 30th. The Queen arrived with a train of Portuguese ladies in their monstrous fardingales, or guard-infantes, their complexions olivader and sufficiently unagreeable. Her Majesty in the same habit, her fore-top long and turned aside very strangely. She was yet of the handsomest countenance of all the rest, and, though low of stature, prettily shaped, languishing and excellent eyes, her teeth wronging her mouth by sticking a little too far out ; for the rest, lovely enough.

" 31st. I saw the Queen at dinner ; the judges came to compliment her arrival, and, after them, the Duke of Ormond brought me to kiss her hand.

" 2nd June. The Lord Mayor and Aldermen made their addresses to the Queen, presenting her 1000l.

in gold. Now saw I her Portuguese ladies, and the Guarda-damas, or Mother of her Maids, and the old knight, a lock of whose hair quite covered the rest of his bald pate, bound on by a thread, very oddly."

Pepys first gives us one of his second hand accounts : " The Queen is brought a few days since to Hampton Court ; and all people say of her to be a very fine and handsome lady, and very discreet ; and that the King is pleased enough with her : which, I fear, will put Madame Castlemaine's nose out of joynt.

He changes his opinion somewhat on having seen the Queen : " Meeting Mr. Pierce, the chyrurgeon, he took me into Somerset House ; and there carried me into the Queen-Mother's presence-chamber, where she was, with our Queen sitting on her left hand, whom I never did see before ; and though she be not very charming, yet she hath a good, modest, and innocent look, which is pleasing."

Of the King's neglect of his wife Pepys bears witness on April 25th, 1663 : " I did hear that the Queen is much grieved of late at the King's neglecting her, he not having supped once with her this quarter of a year, and almost every night with my Lady Castlemaine, who hath been with him this St. George's feast at Windsor, and come home with him last night."

Clarendon is a central figure during the early part of Charles's reign. Pepys's first meeting with him was to explain some misconceptions. This was on July 14th, 1664 :

" So I to my Lord Chancellor's ; and there, coming out after dinner, I accosted him, telling him that I was the unhappy Pepys that had fallen

into his high displeasure, and come to desire him
to give me leave to make myself better understood
to his Lordship, assuring him of my duty and
service. He answered me very pleasingly, that he
was confident upon the score of my Lord Sandwich's character of me, but that he had reason to
think what he did, and desired me to call upon him
some evening : I named to-night, and he accepted
of it. To my Lord Chancellor's, and there heard
several trials, wherein I perceive my Lord is a most
able and ready man. After all done, he himself
called, ' Come, Mr. Pepys, you and I will take a
turn in the garden.' So he was led down stairs,
having the goute, and there walked with me, I
think, above an hour, talking most friendly, yet
cunningly. I told him clearly how things were ;
how ignorant I was of his Lordship's concernment
in it ; how I did not do, nor say, one word singly,
but what was done, was the act of the whole
Board. He told me by name that he was more
angry with Sir G. Carteret than with me, and also
with the whole body of the Board. But, thinking
who it was of the Board that did know him least,
he did place his fear upon me ; but he finds that he
is indebted to none of his friends there. I think I
did thoroughly appease him, till he thanked me
for my desire and pains to satisfy him ; and, upon
my desiring to be directed who I should of his
servants advise with about this business, he told
me nobody, but he would be glad to hear from me
himself. He told me he would not direct me in
anything, that it might not be said that the Lord
Chancellor did labour to abuse the King.''

On April 28th, 1665, the great Lord Chancellor
was quite affectionate : " 28*th*. Down the River,

to visit the victualling-ships, where I find all out of order. And come home to dinner, and then to write a letter to the Duke of Albermarle about them, and carried it myself to the Council-chamber ; and, when they rose, my Lord Chancellor, passing by, stroked me on the head, and told me that the Board had read my letter, and taken order for the punishing of the watermen for not appearing on board the ships. And so did the King afterwards, who do now know me so well, that he never sees me but he speaks to me about our Navy business."

But Pepys is not always reliable for he considered Clarendon at the end of his career in 1663 whereas he continued in office until 1667 : " It seems the present favourites now are my Lord Bristol, Duke of Buckingham, Sir H. Bennet, my Lord Ashley, and Sir Charles Barkeley ; who, among them, have cast my Lord Chancellor upon his back, past ever getting up again ; there being now little for him to do, and he waits at Court attending to speak to the King as others do."

Evelyn's account of the Chancellor's character and fall reads with more conviction : " Visited the Lord Chancellor, to whom his Majesty had sent for the seals a few days before ; I found him in his bed-chamber, very sad. The Parliament had accused him, and he had enemies at Court, especially the buffoons and ladies of pleasure, because he thwarted some of them, and stood in their way ; I could name some of the chief. The truth is, he made few friends during his grandeur among the royal sufferers, but advanced the old rebels. He was, however, though no considerable lawyer, one who kept up the form and substance of things in the Nation with more solemnity than some would have had. He was my particular kind friend, on all occasions. The Cabal, however, prevailed, and that party in Parliament. Great division at Court concerning him, and divers great persons interceding for him. [*August 27th*, 1667.]

In reading Pepys's accounts of General Monk, the man who largely brought about the Restoration, we must be on our guard, for Pepys, a staunch supporter of his patron, Sandwich, was influenced by the latter's prejudices against his rival :

" Thence went and spoke with the Duke of Albemarle about his wound at Newhall, but I find him a heavy dull man, methinks, by his answers to me."

The great Scottish Duke of Lauderdale is amusingly described by Pepys on July 28th, 1666 : " Thence with my Lord to his coach-house, and there put in six horses into his coach, and he and I alone to Highgate. Being come thither, we went to my Lord Lauderdale's house to speak with him, and find him and his lady, and some Scotch people, at supper : pretty odd company, though, my Lord Brouncker tells me, my Lord Lauderdale is a man of mighty good reason and judgement. But at supper there played one of their servants upon the viallin some Scotch tunes only ; several, and the best of their country, as they seemed to esteem them, by their praising and admiring them : but, Lord ! the strangest ayre that ever I heard in my life, and all of one cast. But strange to hear my Lord Lauderdale say himself that he had rather hear a cat mew, than the best musique in the world ; and the better the musique, the more sick it makes him ; and that of all instruments, he hates the lute most, and, next to that, the baggpipe."

The Court.

The Court soon became infamous for its wickedness. There was glamour and Pepys has described the brilliant scene of a dance on November 15th, 1666 : " To Mrs. Pierce's, where I find her as fine as possible, and Mr. Pierce going to the ball at night at Court, it being the Queen's birth-day. I also to the ball, and with much ado got up to the loft, where with much trouble I could see very well. Anon the house grew full, and the candles light, and the King and Queen and all the ladies sat : and it was, indeed, a glorious sight to see Mrs. Stewart in black and white lace, and her head and shoulders dressed with diamonds, and the like many great ladies more, only the Queen none ; and the King in his rich vest of some rich silk and silver trimming, as the Duke of York and all the dancers were, some of cloth of silver, and others of other sorts, exceeding rich. Presently after the King was come in, he took the Queen, and about fourteen more couple there was, and begun the Bransles. . . . After the Bransles, then to a Corant, and now and then a French dance ; but that so rare, that the Corants grew tiresome, that I wished it done. Only Mrs. Stewart danced mighty finely, and many French dances, specially one the King called the New Dance, which was very pretty ; but upon the whole matter, the business of the dancing of itself was not extraordinary pleasing. But the clothes and sight of the persons were indeed very pleasing, and worth my coming, being never likely to see more gallantry while I live, if I should come twenty times. About twelve at night it broke up. So away home with my wife : was displeased with the dull dancing, and satisfied with the clothes and persons. My Lady Castlemaine, without whom all is nothing, being there, very rich, though not dancing."

But the King set the fashion and even loyal Evelyn records his disgust of such a scene as the one he witnessed on March 1st, 1671 : " I thence walked with him through St. James's Park to the garden, where I both saw and heard a very familiar discourse between . . . . . and Mrs. Nelly, as they called an impudent comedian, she looking out of her garden on a terrace at the top of the wall, and . . . . . standing on the green walk under it. I was heartily sorry at this scene. Thence the King walked to the Duchess of Cleveland, another lady of pleasure, and curse of our nation."

Very different is their effect upon Pepys :

" *May 1st*, 1667. To Westminster ; in the way meeting many milk-maids with their garlands upon their pails, dancing with a fiddler before them ; and saw pretty Nelly standing at her lodgings' door in Drury-lane in her smock sleeves and bodice, looking upon one : she seemed a mighty pretty creature.

" *March 1st*, 1663. So I up into the house among the courtiers, seeing the fine ladies, and, above all, my Lady Castlemaine, who is above all, that only she I can observe for true beauty."

Yet even Pepys censures the Court. On February 21st, 1665, he writes : " What mad freaks the Mayds of Honour at Court have : that Mrs. Jenings, one of the Dutchess's maids, the other day dressed herself like an orange wench, and went up and down and cried oranges ; till, falling down, or by some accident, her fine shoes were discerned, and she put to a great deal of shame ; that such as these tricks, being ordinary, and worse among them, thereby few will venture upon them for wives : my Lady Castlemaine will in merriment say, that her daughter, now above a year old or two, will be the first mayd in the Court that will be married."

On August 17th, 1661, he speaks in even stronger terms : " And, in our discourse, he was very forward to complain and to speak loud of the lewdnesse and beggary of the Court, which I am sorry to hear, and which I am afraid will bring all to ruin again."

Such a Court would rejoice at the downfall of honest Clarendon. Of Lady Castlemaine who long ruled the Court, Pepys writes on August 27th, 1667 : " This day, Mr. Pierce, the surgeon, was with me ; and tells me how this business of my Lord Chancellor's was certainly designed in my Lady Castlemaine's chamber ; and that, when he went from the King on Monday morning, she was in bed, though about twelve o'clock, and ran out in her smock into her aviary looking into White Hall garden ; and thither her woman brought her her nightgown ; and stood blessing herself at the old man's going away."

Pepys's news of another courtier, Baptist May, is even more revolting : " He tells me that as soon as Secretary Morrice brought the Great Seale from my Lord Chancellor, Bab. May fell upon his knees, and catched the King about the legs, and joyed him, and said that this was the first time that ever he could call him King of England, being freed from this great man : which was a most ridiculous saying. And he told me that, when first my Lord Gerard, a great while ago, came to the King, and told him that the Chancellor did say openly that the King was a lazy person and not fit to govern, which is now made one of the things in people's mouths against the Chancellor, 'Why,' says the King, 'that is no news, for he hath told me so twenty times, and but the other day he told me so ;' and made matter of mirth at it : but yet this light discourse is likely to prove bad to him.''

But the classic example of this corruption is told by Pepys on June 21st, 1667, when the Dutch were in the Medway burning our Royal Navy : " Sir H. Cholmly come to me this day, and tells me the Court is as mad as ever ; and that the night the Dutch burned our ships the King did sup with my Lady Castlemaine, at the Duchess of Monmouth's, and there were all mad in hunting of a poor moth. All the Court afraid of a Parliament ; but he thinks nothing can save us but the King's giving up all to a Parliament.''

Another extract which cannot be omitted is taken from Evelyn at the close of the reign : " I can never forget the inexpressible luxury and profaneness, gaming, and all dissoluteness, and as it were total forgetfulness of God (it being Sunday evening), which this day se'nnight I was witness of, the King sitting and toying with his concubines, Portsmouth, Cleveland, and Mazarine, etc., a French boy singing love-songs, in that glorious gallery, whilst about twenty of the great courtiers and other dissolute persons were at Basset round a large table, a bank of at least 2000 in gold before them ; upon which two gentlemen who were with me made reflections with astonishment. Six days after, was all in the dust.''

It is a pleasure to turn to Evelyn's entry a few days later, recording a changed if somewhat hypocritical Court : " The King was this night very obscurely buried in a vault under Henry the Seventh's Chapel at Westminster, without any manner of pomp, and soon forgotten after all this vanity, and the face of the whole Court was exceedingly changed into a more solemn and moral behaviour ; the new King affecting neither profaneness nor buffoonery. All the great officers broke their staves over the grave, according to form."

The Coronation of Charles II.

The reign of Charles II. commenced in a fervour of loyalty and both Evelyn and Pepys have given accounts of the Coronation. Although long, they will both be inserted as they well illustrate the contrast between the diarists, Evelyn taking a keen intellectual interest in all the proceedings, while Pepys was present for sightseeing and enjoyment.

Evelyn writes : " 23rd April. Was the Coronation of his Majesty Charles the Second in the Abbey-Church of Westminster ; at all which ceremony I was present. The King and his Nobility went to the Tower, I accompanying my Lord Viscount Mordaunt part of the way ; this was on Sunday, the 22nd, but indeed his Majesty went not till early this morning, and proceeded from thence to Westminster, in this order.

" First, went the Duke of York's Horse Guards. Messengers of the Chamber. 136 Esquires to the Knights of the Bath, each of whom had two most richly habited. The Knight Harbinger. Sergeant Porter. Sewers of the Chamber. Quarter Waiters. Six Clerks of Chancery. Clerk of the Signet. Clerk of the Privy Seal, etc. . . .

" This magnificent train on horseback, as rich as embroidery, velvet, cloth of gold and silver, and jewels, could make them and their prancing horses, proceeded through the streets strewed with flowers, houses hung with rich tapestry, windows and balconies full of ladies ; the London militia lining the ways, and the several companies, with their banners and loud music, ranked in their orders ; the fountains running wine, bells ringing, with speeches made at the several triumphal arches ; at that of the Temple Bar (near which I stood) the Lord Mayor was received by the Bailiff of Westminster, who, in a scarlet robe, made a speech. Thence, with joyful acclamations, his Majesty passed to Whitehall. Bonfires at night.

" The next day, being St. George's, he went by water to Westminster Abbey. When his Majesty was entered, the Dean and Prebendaries brought all the regalia, and delivered them to several noblemen to bear before the King, who met them at the west door of the church, singing an anthem, to the choir. Then, came the peers, in their robes, and coronets in their hands, till his Majesty was placed on a throne elevated before the altar. Afterwards, the Bishop of London (the Archbishop of Canterbury being sick) went to every side of the throne to present the King to the People, asking if they would have him for their King, and do him homage ; at this, they shouted four times ' God save King Charles the Second ! ' Then, an anthem was sung. His Majesty, attended by three Bishops, went up to the altar, and he offered a pall and a pound of gold. Afterwards, he sate down in another chair during the sermon, which was preached by Dr. Morley, Bishop of Worcester.

" After sermon, the King took his oath before the altar to maintain the religion, Magna Charta, and laws of the land. The hymn *Véni S. Sp.* followed, and then the Litany by two Bishops. Then the Archbishop of Canterbury, present but much indisposed and weak, said ' Lift up your hearts ; ' at which, the King rose up, and put off his robes and upper garments, and was in a waistcoat so opened in divers places, that the Archbishop might commodiously anoint him, first in the palms of his hands, when an anthem was sung, and a prayer read ; then, his breast and betwixt the shoulders, bending of both arms ; and, lastly, on the crown of the head, with apposite hymns and prayers at each anointing ; this done, the Dean closed and buttoned up the waistcoat. After which, was a coif put on, and the cobbium, sindon or dalmatic, and over this a super-tunic of cloth of gold, with buskins and sandals of the same, spurs, and the sword : a prayer being first said over it by the Archbishop on the altar, before it was girt on by the Lord Chamberlain. Then, the armill, mantle, &c. Then, the Archbishop placed the crown-imperial on the altar, prayed over it, and set it on his Majesty's head, at which all the Peers put on their coronets. Anthems, and rare music, with lutes, viols, trumpets, organs, and voices, were then heard, and the Archbishop put a ring on his Majesty's finger. The King next offered his sword on the altar, which being re-deemed, was drawn, and borne before him. Then, the Archbishop delivered him the sceptre, with the dove in one hand, and, in the other, the sceptre with the globe. The King, kneeling, the Archbishop pronounced the blessing. His Majesty then ascending again his royal throne, whilst Te Deum was singing, all the Peers did their homage, by every one touching his crown. The Archbishop, and the rest of the Bishops, first kissing the King ; who received the Holy Sacrament, and so disrobed, yet with the crown-imperial on his head, and accompanied with all the nobility in the former order, he went on foot upon blue cloth, which was spread and reached from the west door of the Abbey to Westminster stairs, when he took water in a triumphal barge to Whitehall, where was extraordinary feasting."

Pepys's account runs as follows :

"Coronačon Day.

"23rd. About four I rose and got to the Abbey, where I followed Sir J. Denham, the surveyor, with some company he was leading in. And with much ado, by the favour of Mr. Cooper, his man, did get up into a great scaffold across the North end of the Abbey, where with a great deal of patience I sat from past four till eleven before the King come in. And a great pleasure it was to see the Abbey raised in the middle, all covered with red, and a throne (that is, a chaire) and footstoole on the top of it ; and all the officers of all kinds, so much as the very fiddlers, in red vests. At last comes in the Dean and Prebendaries of Westminster, with the Bishops, (many of them in cloth of gold copes,) and after them the Nobility, all in their Parliament robes, which was a most magnificent sight. Then the Duke, and the King with a sceptre (carried by my Lord Sandwich) and sword and wand before him, and the crowne too. The King in his robes, bare-headed, which was very fine. And after all had placed themselves, there was a sermon and the service; and then in the Quire at the high altar, the King passed through all the ceremonies of the Coronačon, which to my great grief I and most in the Abbey could not see. The crowne being put upon his head, a great shout begun, and he come forth to the throne, and there passed through more ceremonies: as taking the oath, and having things read to him by the Bishopp; and his lords (who put on their caps as soon as the King put on his crowne) and bishops come, and kneeled before him. And three times the King at Armes went to the three open places on the scaffold, and proclaimed, that if any one could show any reason why Charles Stewart should not be King of England, that now he should come and speak. And a Generall Pardon also was read by the Lord Chancellor, and meddalls flung up and down by my Lord Cornwallis, of silver, but I could not come by any. But so great a noise that I could make but little of the musique; and indeed, it was lost to every body. I went out a little while before the King had done all his ceremonies, and went round the Abbey to Westminster Hall, all the way within rayles, and 10,000 people with the ground covered with blue cloth; and scaffolds all the way. Into the Hall I got, where it was very fine with hangings and scaffolds one upon another full of brave ladies; and my wife in one little one, on the right hand. Here I staid walking up and down, and at last upon one of the side stalls I stood and saw the King come in with all the persons (but the soldiers) that were yesterday in the cavalcade; and a most pleasant sight it was to see them in their several robes. And the King come in with his crowne on, and his sceptre in his hand, under a

canopy borne up by six silver staves, carried by
Barons of the Cinque Ports, and little bells at every
end. And after a long time he got up to the farther
end, and all set themselves down at their several
tables ; and that was also a brave sight : and the
King's first course carried up by the Knights of
the Bath. And many fine ceremonies there was
of the Heralds leading up people before him, and
bowing ; and my Lord of Albemarle's going to
the kitchen and eating a bit of the first dish that
was to go to the King's table. But, above all, was
these three Lords, Northumberland, and Suffolke
and the Duke of Ormond, coming before the courses
on horseback, and staying so all dinner-time, and
at last bringing up [Dymock,] the King's Champion, all in armour on horseback, with his speare
and targett carried before him. And a Herald pro-
claims ' That if any dare deny Charles Stuart to be
lawful King of England, here was a Champion that
would fight with him ; ' and with these words, the
Champion flings down his gauntlet, and all this
he do three times in his going up towards the King's
table. To which, when he is come, the King drinks
to him, and then sends him the cup which is of
gold, and he drinks it off, and then rides back
again with the cup in his hand. I went from table
to table to see the Bishops and all others at their
dinner, and was infinitely pleased with it. And at
the Lord's table, I met with William Howe, and
he spoke to my Lord for me, and he did give him
four rabbits and a pullet, and so Mr. Creed and I
got Mr. Minshell to give us some bread, and so
we at a stall eat it, as every body else did what
they could get. I took a great deal of pleasure to
go up and down, and look upon the ladies, and to

hear the musique of all sorts, but above all, the 24 violins."

Punishment of regicides and others.

There is little wonder that, during the wave of loyalty which passed over the country at the Restoration, some of those who were responsible for the death of Charles I. suffered. Pepys, the somewhat heartless busybody, was there to see all the sights :

" I went out to Charing Cross, to see Major-General Harrison hanged, drawn, and quartered ; which was done there, he looking as cheerful as any man could do in that condition. He was presently cut down, and his head and heart shown to the people, at which there was great shouts of joy. It is said, that he said that he was sure to come shortly at the right hand of Christ to judge them that now had judged him ; and that his wife do expect his coming again. Thus it was my chance to see the King beheaded at White Hall, and to see the first blood shed in revenge for the King at Charing Cross.

" This morning, it being expected that Colonel Hacker and Axtell should die, I went to Newgate, but found they were reprieved till to-morrow.

" This morning Mr. Carew was hanged and quartered at Charing Cross, but his quarters, by a great favour, are not to be hanged up." [*September 15th*, 1660.]

Even the dead are dishonoured : " To my Lady Batten's ; where my wife and she are lately come back again from being abroad, and seeing of Cromwell, Ireton, and Bradshaw, hanged and buried at Tyburne."

The more refined Evelyn shrinks from such ghastliness, although in it he sees the hand of Providence at work :

" 11th. The regicides who sat on the life of our late King were brought to trial in the Old Bailey, before a commission of Oyer and Terminer.

" 14th. Axtall, Carew, Clement, Hacker, Hewson, and Peters, were executed.

" 17th. Scot, Scroop, Cook, and Jones, suffered for reward of their iniquities at Charing Cross, in sight of the place where they put to death their natural prince, and in the presence of the King his son, whom they also sought to kill. I saw not their execution, but met their quarters, mangled, and cut, and reeking, as they were brought from the gallows in baskets on the hurdle. Oh, the miraculous providence of God !

" This day (O the stupendous and inscrutable judgments of God !) were the carcases of those arch-rebels, Cromwell, Bradshawe (the judge who condemned his Majesty), and Ireton (son-in-law to the Usurper), dragged out of their superb tombs in Westminster among the Kings, to Tyburn, and hanged on the gallows there from nine in the morning till six at night, and then buried under that fatal and ignominious monument in a deep pit ; thousands of people who had seen them in all their pride being spectators. Look back at October 22, 1658, and be astonished ! and fear God and honour the King ; but meddle not with them who are given to change ! "

These punishments appear brutal to us, but cruelty in those days was of less consequence than is the case now : " Mrs. Anne and I rode under the man that hangs upon Shooter's Hill, and a filthy sight it was to see how his flesh is shrunk to his bones." [Pepys, *April 11th*, 1661.]

" I to Sir G. Carteret's to dinner ; where Mr. Cofferer Ashburnham ; who told a good story of a prisoner's being condemned at Salisbury for a small matter. While he was on the bench with his father-in-law, Judge Richardson, and while they were considering to transport him to save his life, the fellow flung a great stone at the Judge, that missed him, but broke through the wainscoat. Upon this, he had his hand cut off, and was hanged presently." [Pepys, *September 8th*, 1667.]

" I saw one Carr pilloried at Charing Cross for a libel, which was burnt before him by the hangman." [Evelyn, *December 21st*, 1668.]

" Passing by Smithfield, I saw a miserable creature burning, who had murdered her husband." [Evelyn, *May 10th*, 1652.]

In 1652 Evelyn was robbed. His account of the sequel is as follows : " One of the men who robbed me was taken ; I was accordingly summoned to appear against him ; and, on the 12th, was in Westminster Hall, but not being bound over, nor willing to hang the fellow, I did not appear, coming only to save a friend's bail ; but the bill being found, he was turned over to the Old Bailey. In the mean time, I received a petition from the prisoner, whose father I understood was an honest old farmer in Kent. He was charged with other crimes, and condemned, but reprieved. I heard afterwards that, had it not been for his companion, a younger man, he would probably have killed me. He was afterwards charged with some other crime, but, refusing to plead, was pressed to death."

The punishment of Titus Oates, of Popish Plot

fame, strikes us with disgust, however richly
deserved his reward might have been : " Oates,
who had but two days before been pilloried at
several places and whipped at the cart's tail from
Newgate to Aldgate, was this day placed on a
sledge, being not able to go by reason of so late
scourging, and dragged from prison to Tyburn,
and whipped again all the way, which some
thought to be severe and extraordinary ; but, if he
was guilty of the perjuries, and so of the death of
many innocents, (as I fear he was,) his punishment
was but what he deserved. I chanced to pass just
as execution was doing on him. A strange revolution ! " [Evelyn, *June 14th*, 1685.]

But harsh as were our punishments, those abroad
appear to have been worse : " I went to the
Châtelet, or prison, where a malefactor was to have
the question, or torture, given to him, he refusing
to confess the robbery with which he was charged,
which was thus : they first bound his wrist with a
strong rope, or small cable, and one end of it to an
iron ring made fast to the wall, about four feet
from the floor, and then his feet with another
cable, fastened about five feet farther than his
utmost length to another ring on the floor of the
room. Thus suspended, and yet lying but aslant,
they slid a horse of wood under the rope which
bound his feet, which so exceedingly stiffened it,
as severed the fellow's joints in miserable sort,
drawing him out at length in an extraordinary
manner, he having only a pair of linen drawers on
his naked body. Then, they questioned him of a
robbery (the Lieutenant being present, and a clerk
that wrote), which not confessing, they put a
higher horse under the rope, to increase the torture

and extension. In this agony, confessing nothing, the executioner with a horn (just such as they drench horses with) stuck the end of it into his mouth, and poured the quantity of two buckets of water down his throat and over him, which so prodigiously swelled him, as would have pitied and affrighted any one to see it ; for all this, he denied all that was charged to him. They then let him down, and carried him before a warm fire to bring him to himself, being now to all appearance dead with pain. What became of him, I know not ; but the gentleman whom he robbed constantly averred him to be the man, and the fellow's suspicious pale looks, before he knew he should be racked, betrayed some guilt ; the Lieutenant was also of that opinion, and told us at first sight (for he was a lean, dry, black young man) he would conquer the torture ; and so it seems they could not hang him, but did use in such cases, where the evidence is very presumptive, to send them to the galleys, which is as bad as death.

" There was another malefactor to succeed, but the spectacle was so uncomfortable, that I was not able to stay the sight of another. It represented yet to me the intolerable sufferings which our Blessed Saviour must needs undergo, when his body was hanging with all its weight upon the nails on the cross." [Evelyn, *March* 11th, 1651.]

Corruption.

Charles II.'s reign had not proceeded far before it was evident that corruption had set in. Evelyn's loyalty and refinement keep him from saying much about this, but Pepys is ever ready to seek and record news good or bad.

On August 31st, 1661, he writes: "At Court things are in very ill condition, there being so much emulacion, poverty, and the vices of drinking, swearing, and loose amours, that I know not what will be the end of it, but confusion. And the Clergy so high, that all people that I meet with do protest against their practice. In short, I see no content or satisfaction any where, in any one sort of people. . . . We are at our Office quiet, only for lack of money all things go to rack. Our very bills offered to be sold upon the Exchange at 10 per cent. loss."

That bribery was the order of the day was evident from an entry on October 12th, 1663: "At St. James's we attended the Duke all of us. And there, after my discourse, Mr. Coventry of his own accord begun to tell the Duke how he found that discourse abroad did run to his prejudice about the fees that he took, and how he sold places and other things; wherein he desired to appeal to his Highness, whether he did any thing more than what his predecessors did, and appealed to us all. So Sir G. Carteret did answer that some fees were heretofore taken, but what he knows not; only that selling of places never was, nor ought to be, countenanced. So Mr. Coventry very hotly answered to Sir G. Carteret, and appealed to himself whether he was not one of the first that put him upon looking after this business of fees, and that he told him that Mr. Smith should say that he made £5000 the first year, and he believed he made £7000. This Sir Carteret denied, and said, that if he did say so, he told a lie; for he could not, nor did know, that ever he did make that profit of his place; but that he believes he might say £2500 the first year. Mr.

Coventry instanced in another thing, particularly wherein Sir G. Carteret did advise with him about the selling of the Auditor's place of the stores, when in the beginning there was an intention of creating such an office. This he confessed, but with some lessening of the tale Mr. Coventry told, it it being only for a respect to my Lord Fitz Harding. In fine, Mr. Coventry did put into the Duke's hand a list of above 250 places that he did give without receiving one farthing, so much as his ordinary fees for them, upon his life and oath ; and that since the Duke's establishment of fees he had never received one token more of any man ; and that in his whole life he never conditioned or discoursed of any consideration from any commanders since he come to the Navy. And afterwards, my Lord Barkeley merrily discoursing that he wished his [Mr. Coventry] profit greater than it was, and that he did believe that he [Mr. Coventry] had got £50,000 since he come in, Mr. Coventry did openly declare that his Lordship, or any of us, should have, not only all he had got, but all that he had in the world, and yet he did not come a beggar into the Navy, nor would yet be thought to speak in any contempt of his Royall Highness's bounty ; and should have a year to consider of it too, for £25,000. The Duke's answer was, that he wished we all had made more profit than we had of our places, and that we had all of us got as much as one man below stayres in the Court, which he presently named, and it was Sir George Lane."

Pepys records four instances of bribery in as many days and appears to censure the custom : " But, good God ! what an age is this, and what a a world is this ! that a man cannot live without playing the knave and dissimulation." [Pepys, *September 5th*, 1661.]

Yet he is tarred with the same brush. At the same time he bears testimony to the tact and ingenuity of the bribers : " At the Dog Tavern Captain Curle, late of the *Maria*, gave me five pieces in gold and a silver can for my wife, for the commission I did give him this day for his ship, dated April 20, 1660."

" Lady Pickering told me the story of her husband's case, and desired my assistance with my Lord, and did give me, wrapped up in paper, £5 in silver. With my Lord to White Hall, and my Lady Pickering. My Lord went at night with the King to Baynard's Castle to supper, and I home. My wife and the girl and dog came home to-day. I found a quantity of chocolate left for me, I know not from whom." [Pepys, *June 19th*, 1660.]

" *10th February*, 1663. W. Warren come himself to the door, and left a letter and box for me, and went his way. His letter mentions giving me and my wife a pair of gloves ; but, opening the box, we found a pair of plain white gloves for my hand, and a fair state-dish of silver, and cup, with my armes, ready cut, upon them, worth, I believe, about £18, which is a very noble present, and the best I ever had yet."

" To the 'Change, and thence off to the Sun Taverne with Sir W. Warren. He did give me a pair of gloves for my wife wrapt up in a paper, which I would not open, feeling it hard ; but did tell him that my wife should thank him, and so went on in discourse. When I come home, Lord ! in what pain I was to get my wife out of the room without bidding her go, that I might see what these gloves were ; and, by and by, she being gone, it proves a pair of white gloves for her, and forty pieces in good gold, which did so cheer my heart, that I could eat no victuals almost for dinner. I was at a great loss what to do, whether to tell my wife of of it or no, for fear of making her think me to be in a better condition, or in a better way of getting money, than yet I am." [Pepys, *February 2nd*, 1664.]

There was money in the country but Charles and his government could not get sufficient. Funds did not always reach the goal for which they were intended. On 29th February, 1664, Sir Philip Warwick tells Pepys : "That the £1,200,000, which the Parliament with so much ado did first vote to the King, and since hath been re-examined by several committees of the present Parliament, is yet above £300,000 short of making up really to the King the £1,200,000, as by particulars he showed me."

But the King could not keep hold of the money that did reach him. On October 10th, 1666, Pepys has a notable entry concerning the King's accounts :

" They say the King hath had towards this war expressly thus much :—

Royal Ayde	£2,450,000
More	1,250,000
Three months' tax given the King by a power of raising a month's tax of £70,000 every year for three years .	0,210,000
Customes, out of which the King did promise to pay £240,000, which, for two years, come to . . .	0,480,000
Prizes, which they moderately reckon at	0,300,000

A debt declared by the Navy, by us . <u>0,900,000</u>

                                  5,590,000

The whole charge of the Navy, as we
state it for two years and a month,
hath been but   3,200,000

So what has become of all this sum ?   £2,390,000."

The money was squandered with the result that
some one had to suffer : "*September 2nd*, 1667.
After dinner comes in Mr. Townsend : and there
I was witness of a horrid rateing, which Mr. Ashburnham, as one of the Grooms of the King's Bed-
chamber, did give him for want of linen for the
King's person ; which he swore was not to be
endured, and that the King would not endure it,
and that the King, his father, would have hanged
his Wardrobe-man should he have been served so ;
the King having at this day no hankerchers, and but
three bands to his neck, he swore. Mr. Townsend
pleaded want of money and the owing of the linen-
draper £5000 ; and that he hath of late got many
rich things made—beds, and sheets, and saddles,
without money, and that he can go no further :
but still this old man, indeed, like an old loving
servant, did cry out for the King's person to be
neglected. But, when he was gone, Townsend told
me that it is the grooms taking away the King's
linen at the quarter's end, as their fee, which makes
this great want : for, whether the King can get it or
no, they will run away at the quarter's end with what
he hath had, let the King get more as he can."

"*April 22nd*, 1667. The King was vexed the
other day for having no paper laid for him at the
Council-table, as was usual ; and Sir Richard

Browne did tell his Majesty he would call the person whose work it was to provide it : who being come, did tell his Majesty that he was but a poor man, and was out £400 or £500 for it, which was as much as he is worth ; and that he cannot provide it any longer without money, having not received a penny since the King's coming in."

Charles's shortage of money made him sometimes sympathetic to others in similar circumstances. He permitted one of his subjects to repair his fortunes by a lottery. Pepys gives picturesque details of it on July 20th, 1664 : " To White Hall, to the Committee for Fishing ; but nothing done, it being a great day to-day there upon drawing at the Lottery of Sir Arthur Slingsby. I got in, and stood by the two Queens and the Duchess of York, and just behind my Lady Castlemaine, whom I do heartily admire ; and good sport to see how most that did give their ten pounds did go away with a pair of gloves only for their lot, and one gentlewoman, one Mrs. Fish, with the only blanke. And one I staid to see draw a suit of hangings valued at £430, and they say are well worth the money, or near it. One other suit there is better than that ; but very many lots of three and fourscore pounds. I observed the King and Queen did get but as poor lots as any else. But the wisest man I met with was Mr. Cholmley, who insured as many as would, from drawing of the one blank for 12*d*. ; in which case there was the whole number of persons to one, which, I think, was three or four hundred. And so he insured about 200 for 200 shillings, so that he could not have lost if one of them had drawn it ; for there was enough to pay the £10, but it happened another drew it, and so he got all the money he took."

Evelyn saw the action in its true light : " To London, to see the event of the lottery which his Majesty had permitted Sir Arthur Slingsby to set up for one day in the Banqueting-House, at Whitchall ; I gaining only a trifle, as well as did the King, Queen-Consort, and Queen-Mother, for near thirty lots ; which was thought to be contrived very unhandsomely by the master of it, who was, in truth, a mere shark."

Much is expected of a monarch. We are surprised to learn what Pepys demanded : " In the afternoon I went upon the river : it raining hard upon the water, I put ashore and sheltered myself, while the King come by in his barge, going down towards the Downes to meet the Queen : the Duke being gone yesterday. But methought it lessened my esteem of a king, that he should not be able to command the rain." [Pepys, *July 19th*, 1662.]

The Dutch War.

Charles II.'s policy was far from satisfying the people. His conduct of foreign affairs especially gave dissatisfaction. The Dutch War from 1665 to 1667 can be taken as an illustration of this and we are particularly indebted to Pepys for accounts of it. As the " right hand of the Navy " our diarist was keenly interested in this naval war and bitterly disappointed at the defeats, though these could not be laid to his charge. At first there was a victory to record and Pepys does not forget the gruesome details :

" VICTORY OVER THE DUTCH, JUNE 3, 1665.

" This day they engaged : the Dutch neglecting greatly the opportunity of the wind they had of us ; by which they lost the benefit of their fire-ships.

The Earl of Falmouth, Muskerry, and Mr. Richard Boyle killed on board the Duke's ship, the *Royall Charles*, with one shot : their blood and brains flying in the Duke's face ; and the head of Mr. Boyle striking down the Duke, as some say. Earl of Marlborough, Portland, Rear Admirall Sansum, to Prince Rupert, killed, and Captain Kirby and Ableson. Sir John Lawson wounded on the knee : hath had some bones taken out, and is likely to be well again. Upon receiving the hurt, he sent to the Duke for another to command the *Royall Oake*. The Duke sent Jordan out of the *St. George*, who did brave things in her. Captain Jeremiah Smith, of the *Mary*, was second to the Duke, and stepped between him and Captain Seaton, of the *Urania*, 76 guns and 400 men, who had sworn to board the Duke ; killed him 200 men, and took the ship ; himself losing 99 men, and never an officer saved but himself and lieutenant. His master indeed is saved, with his leg cut off. Admirall Opdam blown up, Trump killed, and said by Holmes ; all the rest of their admiralls, as they say, but Everson, whom they dare not trust for his affection to the Prince of Orange, are killed : we have taken and sunk, as is believed, about twenty-four of their best ships ; killed and taken near 8 or 10,000 men, and lost, we think, not above 700. A greater victory never known in the world. They are all fled ; some 43 got into the Texell, and others elsewhere, and we in pursuit of the rest. Thence, with my heart full of joy, home : then to my Lady Pen's, where they are all joyed, and not a little puffed up at the good success of their father ; and good service indeed is said to have been done by him. Had a great bonfire at the gate ; and I, with my Lady Pen's people and others, to Mrs. Turner's great room, and there down into the street. I did give the boys 4s. among them, and mighty merry : so home to bed, with my heart at great rest and quiet, saving that the consideration of the victory is too great for me presently too comprehend.''

In the next year we were almost defeated off the Downs. Pepys brings two sailors to tell the story to the King :

'' How we found the Dutch fleete at anchor on Friday, half seas over, between Dunkirke and Ostend, and made them slip their anchors. They about ninety, and we less than sixty. We fought them, and put them to the run, till they met with about sixteen sail of fresh ships, and so bore up again. The fight continued till night, and then again the next morning, from five till seven at night. And so, too, yesterday morning they begun again, and continued till about four o'clock, they chasing us for the most part of Saturday, and yesterday we flying from them. The Duke himself, and then those people who were put into the catch, by and by spied the Prince's fleete coming, upon which De Ruyter called a little council, being in chase at this time of us, and thereupon their fleete divided into two squadrons ; forty in one, and about thirty in the other, the fleete being at first about ninety, but, by one accident or other, supposed to be lessened to about seventy ; the bigger to follow the Duke, the less to meet the Prince. But the Prince come up with the Generall's fleete, and the Dutch come together again, and bore towards their own coast, and we with them ; and now what the consequence of this day will

be, we know not. The Duke was forced to come to
anchor on Friday, having lost his sails and rigging.
No particular person spoken of to be hurt but Sir
W. Clerke, who hath lost his leg, and bore it bravely.
The Duke himself had a little hurt in his thigh,
but signified little. The King did pull out of his
pocket about twenty pieces in gold, and did give
it Daniel for himself and his companion ; and so
parted, mightily pleased with the account he did
give him of the fight, and the success it ended
with, of the Prince's coming, though it seems the
Duke did give way again and again. The King
did give order for care to be had of Mr. Daniel and
his companion ; and so we parted from him, and
then met the Duke of York, and gave him the
same account : and so broke up, and I left them
going to the surgeon's."

Pepys shrewdly diagnoses the cause of our ill-
success in the later part of the war. Lack of money
crippled everything. Sailors were discharged with
tickets instead of ready money and it was found
difficult to convert these tickets into gold. Pepys
successfully defended the Navy Board when
charged in Parliament with these abuses. The
press-gang, too, was a great cause of trouble. Little
wonder that the personnel of the Navy left much
to be desired : "Want of money in the Navy
puts everything out of order. Men grow mutinous ;
and nobody here to mind the business of the Navy
but myself." [31st October, 1665.]

"Did business, though not much, at the office,
because of the horrible crowd and lamentable moan
of the poor seamen, that lie starving in the streets
for lack of money, which do trouble and perplex
me to the heart ; and more at noon, when we were

to go through them, for then above a whole hundred of them followed us ; some cursing, some swearing, and some praying to us." [*7th October*, 1665.]

" After dinner, to the office, and much troubled to have 100 seamen all the afternoon there, swearing below, and cursing us, and breaking the glasse windows, and swear they will pull the house down on Tuesday next. I sent word of this to Court, but nothing will help it but money and a rope. [4th *November*, 1665.]

" With these thoughts I lay troubling myself till six o'clock, restless, and at last getting my wife to talk to me to comfort me, which she at last did, and made me resolve to quit my hands of this Office, and endure the trouble no longer than till I can clear myself of it. So with great trouble, but yet with some ease, from this discourse with my wife, I up, and at my Office, whither come my clerks, and so I did huddle the best I could some more notes for my discourse to-day, and by nine o'clock was ready, and did go down to the Old Swan, and there by boat, with T. Harvey and W. Hewer with me, to Westminster, where I found myself come time enough, and my brethren all ready. But I full of thoughts and trouble touching the issue of this day ; and, to comfort myself, did go to the Dog and drink half-a-pint of mulled sack, and in the Hall [Westminster] did drink a dram of brandy at Mrs. Hewlett's ; and with the warmth of this did find myself in better order as to courage, truly. So we all up to the lobby ; and, between eleven or twelve o'clock, were called in, with the mace before us, into the House, where a mighty full House : and we stood at the bar, namely, Brouncker, Sir J. Minnes, Sir T. Harvey, and

myself, W. Pen being in the House, as a Member.
I perceive the whole House was full of expectation
of our defence what it would be, and with great
prejudice. After the Speaker had told us the
dissatisfaction of the House, and read the Report
of the Committee, I began our defence most accep-
tably and smoothly, and continued at it without
any hesitation or losse, but with full scope, and
all my reason free about me, as if it had been at
my own table, from that time till passed three in
the afternoon ; and so ended, without any interruption from the Speaker ; but we withdrew.
And there all my Fellow-Officers, and all the world
that was within hearing, did congratulate me, and
cry up my speech as the best thing they ever heard ;
and my Fellow-Officers were overjoyed in it ;
and we were called in again by and by to answer
only one question, touching our paying tickets to
ticket-mongers ; and so out." [*5th March,* 1668.]

" I did out of my own purse disburse £15 to pay
for their pressing, and diet last night and this
morning ; which is a thing worth record of my
Lord Mayor. Busy about this all the morning,
and about the getting off men pressed by our
officers of the fleete into the service." [*31st June,*
1666.]

" To the Tower several times, about the business
of the pressed men, and late at it till twelve at
night, shipping of them. But, Lord ! how some poor
women did cry ; and in my life I never did see
such natural expression of passion as I did here,
in some women's bewailing themselves, and running
to every parcel of men that were brought, one after
another, to look for their husbands, and wept
over every vessel that went off, thinking they

might be there, and looking after the ship as far as ever they could by moone-light, that it grieved me to the heart to hear them. Besides, to see poor, patient, labouring men and housekeepers, leaving poor wives and families, taken up on a sudden by strangers, was very hard, and that without press-money, but forced against all law to be gone. It is a great tyranny." [*1st July*, 1666.]

"Up, and to the Office; whence Lord Brouncker, J. Minnes, W. Pen, and I went to examine some men that are put in there, for rescuing of men that were pressed into the service: and we do plainly see that the desperate condition that we put men into for want of their pay makes them mad, they being as good men as ever were in the world, and would as readily serve the King again, were they but paid. Two men leapt overboard—among others, into the Thames, out of the vessel into which they were pressed, and were shot by the soldiers placed there to keep them, two days since; so much people do avoid the King's service! And then these men are pressed without money, and so we cannot punish them for any thing, so that we are forced only to make a show of severity by keeping them in prison, but are unable to punish them." [*22nd August*, 1667.]

With the Navy in this state we are not surprised to find the Dutch able to sail up the Thames, break the boom across the river and even capture some of the Royal Navy lying idle in Chatham owing to lack of money. Pepys views this incident largely from the point of view of its effect on those in charge of the Navy.

On 10th June, 1667: "The Dutch are fallen down from the Hope and Shell-haven as low as

Sheernesse, and we do plainly at this time hear the guns play."

"Home, where all our hearts do now ake; for the news is true, that the Dutch have broke the chaine and burned our ships, and particularly the *Royal Charles*; other particulars I know not, but it is said to be so." [*12th June*, 1667.]

"But that, that he tells me of worst consequence is, that he himself, I think he said, did hear many Englishmen on board the Dutch ships speaking to one another in English; and that they did cry and say, 'We did heretofore fight for tickets; now we fight for dollars!' and did ask how such and such a one did, and would commend themselves to them: which is a sad consideration . . . And indeed the hearts as well as affections of the seamen are turned away; and in the open streets in Wapping, and up and down, the wives have cried publickly, 'This comes of your not paying our husbands; and now your work is undone, or done by hands that understand it not.' And Sir W. Batten told me that he was himself affronted with a woman, in language of this kind, on Tower Hill publickly yesterday; and we are fain to bear it, and to keep one at the office-door to let no idle people in, for fear of firing of the office and doing us mischief." [*14th June*, 1667.]

So serious was the situation that soldiers had to be sent to meet a possible invasion: "Down to Blackewall, and there saw the soldiers, who were by this time gotten most of them drunk, shipped off. But, Lord! to see how the poor fellows kissed their wives and sweethearts in that simple manner at their going off, and shouted, and let off their guns, was strange sport."

Pepys was generous enough to pay the Dutch a compliment : " It seems very remarkable to me, and of great honour to the Dutch, that those of them that did go on shore to Gillingham, though they went in fear of their lives, and were some of them killed ; and, notwithstanding their provocation at Schelling, yet killed none of our people nor plundered their houses, but did take some things of easy carriage, and left the rest, and not a house burned." [*30th June*, 1667.]

Evelyn, although professionally interested in this attack—he was a commissioner for attending to the sick and wounded—takes a rather broader view than that of his fellow-diarist, and thinks of the national disgrace :

" *June 8th*. To London, alarmed by the Dutch, who were fallen on our fleet at Chatham, by a most audacious enterprise entering the very river with part of their fleet, doing us not only disgrace, but incredible mischief in burning several of our best men-of-war lying at anchor and moored there, and all this through our unaccountable negligence in not setting out our fleet in due time. This alarm caused me, fearing the enemy might venture up the Thames even to London (which they might have done with ease, and fired all the vessels in the River, too), to send away my best goods, plate, &c., from my house to another place. The alarm was so great that it put both Country and City into fear, a panic, and consternation, such as I hope I shall never see more ; everybody was flying, none knew why or whither. Now, there were land-forces despatched with the Duke of Albemarle, Lord Middleton, Prince Rupert, and the Duke, to hinder the Dutch coming to Chatham, fortifying Upnor

Castle, and laying chains and bombs; but the resolute enemy brake through all, and set fire on our ships, and retreated in spite, stopping up the Thames, the rest of the fleet lying before the mouth of it."

"14th. I went to see the work at Woolwich, a battery to prevent them coming up to London, which Prince Rupert commanded, and sunk some ships in the river.

"17th. This night, about two o'clock, some chips and combustible matter prepared for some fire-ships, taking flame in Deptford-yard, made such a blaze, and caused such an uproar in the Tower (it being given out that the Dutch fleet was come up, and had landed their men and fired the Tower), as had liked to have done more mischief before people would be persuaded to the contrary and believe the accident. Everybody went to their arms. These were sad and trouble-some times."

"28th. I went to Chatham, and thence to view not only what mischief the Dutch had done; but how triumphantly their whole fleet lay within the very mouth of the Thames, all from the North Fore-land, Margate, even to the buoy of the Nore—a dreadful spectacle as ever Englishmen saw, and a dishonour never to be wiped off! Those who ad-vised his Majesty to prepare no fleet this spring deserved—I know what—but——

Here in the river off Chatham, just before the town, lay the carcase of the *London* (now the third time burnt), the *Royal Oak*, the *James*, &c. yet smoking; and now, when the mischief was done, we were making trifling forts on the brink of the river."

The Plague.

National disasters in the shape of the Plague and Great Fire of London came to add their quota to the difficulties of those to whose hands the government was entrusted. Both diarists gallantly stuck to their tasks in London during the Plague which raged during the latter half of the year 1665. As will readily be imagined the curious Pepys is keenly and sometimes morbidly interested in the Plague, and he gives us minute details revealing his own attitude and the effects on the life of the times.

"The hottest day that ever I felt in my life. This day, much against my will, I did in Drury Lane see two or three houses marked with a red cross upon the doors, and 'Lord have mercy upon us!' writ there; which was a sad sight to me, being the first of the kind that, to my remembrance, I ever saw. It put me into an ill conception of myself and my smell, so that I was forced to buy some roll-tobacco to smell to and chaw, which took away the apprehension." [*7th June*, 1665.]

"By and by met my Lord Crewe returning; Mr. Marr telling me, by the way, how a maid servant of Mr. John Wright's, who lives thereabouts, falling sick of the plague, she was removed to an outhouse, and a nurse appointed to look to her; who, being once absent, the maid got out of the house at the window, and run away. The nurse coming and knocking, and, having no answer, believed she was dead, and went and told Mr. Wright so; who and his lady were in great straight what to do to get her buried. At last, resolved to go to Burntwood, hard by, being in the parish, and there get people to do it. But they would not:

so he went home full of trouble, and in the way
met the wench walking over the common, which
frightened him worse than before; and was
forced to send people to take her, which he did;
and they got one of the pest-coaches, and put her
into it, to carry her to a pest-house. And, passing
in a narrow lane, Sir Anthony Browne, with his
brother and some friends in the coach, met this
coach with the curtains drawn close. The brother,
being a young man, and believing there might
be some lady in it that would not be seen, and the
way being narrow, he thrust his head out of his
own into her coach, and to look, and there saw
somebody looking very ill, and in a silk dress,
and stunk mightily; which the coachman also
cried out upon. And presently they come up to
some people that stood looking after it, and told
our gallants that it was a maid of Mr. Wright's
carried away sick of the plague; which put the
young gentleman into a fright had almost cost him
his life, but is now well again." [*3rd August*, 1665.]

" By and by to the office, where we sat all the
morning; in great trouble to see the Bill this week
rise so high, to above 4000 in all, and of them
above 3000 of the plague. Home, to draw over
anew my will, which I had bound myself by oath
to dispatch by tomorrow night; the town growing
so unhealthy, that a man cannot depend upon
living two days." [*10th August*, 1665.]

" The people die so, that now it seems they are
fain to carry the dead to be buried by daylight,
the nights not sufficing to do it in. And my Lord
Mayor commands people to be within at nine at
night all, as they say, that the sick may have
liberty to go abroad for ayre. There is one also

dead out of one of our ships at Deptford, which
troubles us mightily—the *Providence*, fire-ship,
which was just fitted to go to sea; but they tell
me, to-day, no more sick on board. And this day
W. Bodham tells me that one is dead at Woolwich,
not far from the Rope-yard. I am told, too, that
a wife of one of the groomes at Court is dead at
Salisbury; so that the King and Queen are speedily
to be all gone to Wilton. So God preserve us!"
[12*th August*, 1665.]

"I went forth, and walked towards Moorefields
to see, God forgive my presumption! whether I
could see any dead corpse going to the grave;
but, as God would have it, did not. But, Lord!
how every body's looks, and discourse in the street,
is of death, and nothing else; and few people going
up and down, that the town is like a place distressed and forsaken." [30*th August*, 1665.]

"Up; and, after putting several things in order
to my removal, to Woolwich; the plague having a
great encrease this week, beyond all expectation,
of almost 2000, making the general Bill 7000, odd
100; and the plague above 6000. Thus this month
ends with great sadness upon the publick, through
the greatness of the plague everywhere through the
kingdom almost. Every day sadder and sadder
news of its encrease. In the City died this week
7496, and of them 6102 of the plague. But it is
feared that the true number of the dead this week
is near 10,000; partly from the poor that cannot be
taken notice of, through the greatness of the
number, and partly from the Quakers and others
that will not have any bell ring for them." [31*st
August*, 1665.]

"I spent some thoughts upon the occurrences

of this day, giving matter for as much content on one hand, and melancholy on another, as any day in all my life. For the first ; the finding of my money and plate, and all safe at London, and speeding in my business this day. The hearing of this good news to such excess, after so great a despair of my Lord's doing any thing this year ; adding to that, the decrease of 500 and more, which is the first decrease we have yet had in the sickness since it begun ; and great hopes that the next week it will be greater. Then, on the other side, my finding that though the Bill in general is abated, yet the City, within the walls, is encreased, and likely to continue so, and is close to our house there. My meeting dead corpses of the plague, carried to be buried close to me at noon-day through the City in Fenchurch Street. To see a person sick of the sores carried close by me by Grace-church in a hackney-coach. My finding the Angel tavern, at the lower end of Tower Hill, shut up ; and more than that, the alehouse at the Tower Stairs ; and more than that, that the person was then dying of the plague when I was last there, a little while ago, at night. To hear that poor Payne, my waiter, hath buried a child, and is dying himself. To hear that a labourer I sent but the other day to Dagenhams, to know how they did there, is dead of the plague ; and that one of my own watermen, that carried me daily, fell sick as soon as he had landed me on Friday morning last, when I had been all night upon the water, and I believe he did get his infection that day at Branford, and is now dead of the plague. To hear that Captain Lambert and Cuttle are killed in the taking these ships ; and that Mr. Sidney Montagu is sick of a desperate fever at my Lady Carteret's, at Scott's Hall. To hear that Mr. Lewes hath another daughter sick. And, lastly, that both my servants, W. Hewer, and Tom Edwards, have lost their fathers, both in St. Sepulchre's parish, of the plague this week, do put me into great apprehensions of melancholy, and with good reason. But I put off my thoughts of sadness as much as I can, and the rather to keep my wife in good heart, and family also." [*14th September*, 1665.]

" But, Lord ! what a sad time it is to see no boats upon the river ; and grass grows all up and down Whitehall court, and nobody but poor wretches in the streets ! And, which is worst of all, the Duke showed us the number of the plague this week, brought in the last night from the Lord Mayor ; that it is encreased about 600 more than the last, which is quite contrary to our hopes and expectations, from the coldness of the late season. For the whole general number is 8297, and of them the plague 7165 ; which is more in the whole, by above 50, than the biggest Bill yet : which is very grievous to us all." [*20th September*, 1665.]

With the colder weather, the Plague began to die down and activities recommenced though progress was slow for the effects of the ravages were to be met with on all sides : " The 'Change pretty full, and the town begins to be lively again, though the streets very empty, and most shops shut." [*26th October*, 1665.]

" Great joy we have this week in the weekly Bill, it being come to 544 in all and but 333 of the plague ; so that we are encouraged to get to London soon as we can. And my father writes as great news of joy to them, that he saw York's waggon go again this week to London, and full of passengers ; and tells me that my aunt Bell hath been dead of the plague these seven weeks." [*30th November*, 1665.]

" I with my Lord Brouncker and Mrs. Williams by coach with four horses to London, to my Lord's house in Covent Garden. But, Lord ! what staring to see a nobleman's coach come to town ! And porters every where bow to us ; and such begging of beggars ! And delightful it is to see the town full of people again ; and shops begin to open, though in many places seven or eight together, and more, all shut ; but yet the town is full, compared with what it used to be. I mean the City end : for Covent Garden and Westminster are yet very empty of people, no Court nor gentry being there." [*5th January*, 1666.]

Lacking the somewhat morbid curiosity of Pepys, Evelyn gives very little concerning the Plague beyond a few numerical details. But one extract reveals the fact that, like his fellow-diarist, he was not only sticking to his task, but was also trying to help in tackling the problem of the scourge : " Came home, there perishing near 17,000 poor creatures weekly ; however, I went all along the city and suburbs from Kent Street to St. James's, a dismal passage, and dangerous to see so many coffins exposed in the streets, now thin of people ; the shops shut up, and all in mournful silence, not knowing whose turn it might be next. I went to the Duke of Albemarle for a pest-ship, to wait on our infected men, who were not a few." [*7th September*, 1665.]

" To London, and went through the whole City, having occasion to alight out of the coach in several places about business of money, when I was environed with multitudes of poor pestiferous creatures begging alms: the shops universally shut up, a dreadful prospect!" [*11th October, 1665.*]

The Fire.

The Great Fire of London which broke out on 2nd September, 1666, gave Pepys an excellent opportunity of exercising his powers of description. He has given us a living account of this disaster, and we note with interest that he is not merely a sightseer. It was he who proposed to the King a practical method of checking the fire. At the same time Pepys was not without anxiety on behalf of his own possessions and his choice of goods to be saved reveals much of Pepys, the man.

" *2nd* (Lord's Day). Some of our maids sitting up late last night to get things ready against our feast to-day, Jane called us up about three in the morning, to tell us of a great fire they saw in the City. So I rose, and slipped on my night-gown, and went to her window: and thought it to be on the back-side of Marke lane at the farthest, but being unused to such fires as followed, I thought it far enough off; and so went to bed again, and to sleep. About seven rose again to dress myself, and there looked out at the window, and saw the fire not so much as it was, and further off. So to my closet to set things to rights, after yesterday's cleaning. By and by Jane comes and tells me that she hears that above 300 houses have been burned down to-night by the fire we saw, and that it is now burning down all Fish street, by London Bridge. So I made myself ready presently, and walked to the Tower, and there got up upon one of the high places, Sir J. Robinson's little son going up with me ; and there I did see the houses at that end of the bridge all on fire, and an infinite great fire on this and the other side the end of the bridge ; which, among other people, did trouble me for poor little Michell and our Sarah on the bridge.

" So down with my heart full of trouble to the Lieutenant of the Tower, who tells me that it begun this morning in the King's baker's house in Pudding-lane, and that it hath burned down St. Magnes Church and most part of Fish-street already. So I down to the water side, and there got a boat, and through bridge, and there saw a lamentable fire. Poor Michell's house, as far as the Old Swan, already burned that way, and the fire running further, that in a very little time it got as far as the Steele-yard, while I was there. Every body endeavouring to remove their goods, and flinging into the river or bringing them into lighters that lay off ; poor people staying in their houses as long as till the very fire touched them, and then running into boats, or clambering from one pair of stairs by the water side to another. And among other things, the poor pigeons, I perceive, were loth to leave their houses, but hovered about the windows and balconys, till they burned their wings, and fell down.

" Having staid, and in an hour's time seen the fire rage every way, and nobody, to my sight, endeavouring to quench it, but to remove their goods, and leave all to the fire, and having seen it get as far as the Steele-yard, and the wind mighty high, and driving it into the City : and every thing after so long a drought proving combustible, even the very stones of churches, and among other things, the poor steeple by which pretty Mrs.—— lives, and whereof my old school-fellow Elborough is parson, taken fire in the very top, and there burned till it fell down ; I to White Hall (with a gentleman with me, who desired to go off from the Tower, to see the fire, in my boat) : and there up to the King's closet in the Chapel, where people come about me, and I did give them an account dismayed them all, and word was carried in to the King. So I was called for, and did tell the King and Duke of York what I saw, and that unless his Majesty did command houses to be pulled down, nothing could stop the fire. They seemed much troubled, and the King commanded me to go to my Lord Mayor from him, and command him to spare no houses, but to pull down before the fire every way. The Duke of York bid me tell him, that if he would have any more soldiers, he shall : and so did my Lord Arlington afterwards, as a great secret.

" Here meeting with Captain Cocke, I in his coach, which he lent me, and Creed with me to Paul's, and there walked along Watling-street, as well as I could, every creature coming away loaded with goods to save, and here and there sick people carried away in beds. Extraordinary good goods carried in carts and on backs. At last met my Lord Mayor in Canning-street, like a man spent, with a handkercher about his neck. To the King's message, he cried, like a fainting woman, ' Lord ! what can I do ? I am spent : people will not obey me. I have been pulling down houses ; but the fire overtakes us faster than we can do it.' That he needed no more soldiers ; and that, for himself, he must go and refresh himself, having been up all night.

" So he left me, and I him, and walked home ; seeing people all almost distracted, and in no manner of means used to quench the fire. The houses too so very thick thereabouts, and full of matter for burning, as pitch and tar, in Thames street ; and warehouses of oyle, and wines, and brandy, and other things. . . . River full of lighters ; and boats taking in goods, and good goods swimming in the water and only I observed that hardly one lighter or boat in three that had the goods of a house in, but there was a pair of Virginalls in it. Having seen as much as I could now, I away to Whitehall by appointment, and there walked to St. James's Park, and there met my wife and Creed and Wood and his wife, and walked to my boat ; and there upon the water again, and to the fire up and down, it still encreasing, and the wind great. So near the fire as we could for smoke ; and all over the Thames, with one's faces in the wind, you were almost burned with a shower of fire-drops. This is very true : so as houses were burned by these drops and flakes of fire, three or four, nay, five or six houses, one from another.

" When we could endure no more upon the water, we to a little ale house on the Bankside, over against the Three Cranes, and there staid till it was dark almost, and saw the fire grow, and as it grew darker, appeared more and more, and in corners and upon steeples, and between churches and houses, as far as we could see up the hill of the City, in a most horrid malicious bloody flame, not like the fine flame of an ordinary fire. Barbary and her husband away before us. We staid till it being darkish, we saw the fire as only one entire arch of fire from this to the other side the bridge, and in a bow up the hill for an arch of above a mile long ; it made me weep to see it. The churches, houses, and all on fire, and flaming at once ; and a horrid noise the flames made, and the cracking of houses at their ruine.

" 3*rd*. About four o'clock in the morning, my Lady Batten sent me a cart to carry away all my money, and plate, and best things, to Sir W. Rider's at Bednall-greene. Which I did, riding myself in my night-gown, in the cart ; and, Lord ! to see how the streets and the highways are crowded with people running and riding, and getting of carts at any rate to fetch away things.

. . . " 4*th*. Sir W. Batten not knowing how to remove his wine, did dig a pit in the garden, and laid it in there ; and I took the opportunity of laying all the papers of my office that I could not otherwise dispose of. And in the evening Sir W. Pen and I did dig another, and put our wine in it ; and I my parmazan cheese, as well as my wine and some other things. . . .

" This night Mrs. Turner (who, poor woman, was removing her goods all this day, good goods into the garden, and knows not how to dispose of them), and her husband supped with my wife and me at night, in the office, upon a shoulder of mutton from the cook's, without any napkin, or any thing, in a sad manner, but were merry. Only now and then, walking into the garden, saw how horribly the sky looks, all on a fire in the night, was enough to put us out of our wits ; and, indeed, it was extremely dreadful for it looks just as if it was at us, and the whole heaven on fire.

" I after supper walked in the dark down to Tower-street, and there saw it all on fire, at the Trinity House on that side, and the Dolphin Tavern on this side, which was very near us ; and the fire with extraordinary vehemence. Now begins the practice of blowing up of houses in Tower-street, those next the Tower, which at first did frighten people more than any thing ; but it stopped the fire where it was done, it bringing down the houses to the ground in the same places they stood, and then it was easy to quench what little fire was in it, though it kindled nothing almost.

" 5*th*. I lay down in the office again upon W. Hewer's quilt, being mighty weary, and sore in my feet with going till I was hardly able to stand. About two in the morning my wife calls me up, and tells me of new cryes of fire, it being come to Barking Church, which is the bottom of our lane. I up ; and finding it so, resolved presently to take her away, and did, and took my gold, which was about 2350*l*., W. Hewer, and Jane, down of Proundy's boat to Woolwich ; but Lord ! what a sad sight it was by moone-light to see the whole City almost on fire, that you might see it as plain at Woolwich, as if you were by it. There, when I come, I find the gates shut, but no guard kept at all ; which troubled me, because of discourses now begun, that there is a plot in it, and that the French had done it. I got the gates open, and to Mr. Shelden's, where I locked up my gold, and charged my wife and W. Hewer never to leave the room without one of them in it, night or day. So back again, by the way seeing my goods well in the lighters at Dept-ford, and watched well by people.

" 16*th March*, 1667. The weather is now grown

warm again, after much cold ; and it is observable
that within these eight days I did see smoke remaining, coming out of some cellars from the late
great fire, now above six months since."

Evelyn's account is more scholarly, objective
and comprehensive. We should look in vain to
Evelyn for an account similar to that of Pepys
burying his wine, but the description is nevertheless
interesting and useful.

" *2nd September*. This fatal night, about ten,
began the deplorable fire, near Fish-street, in
London.

" *3rd*. I had public prayers at home. The fire
continuing, after dinner, I took coach with my
wife and son, and went to the Bankside in Southwark, where we beheld that dismal spectacle, the
whole city in dreadful flames near the waterside ;
all the houses from the Bridge, all Thames-street,
and upwards towards Cheapside, down to the Three
Cranes, were now consumed ; and so returned,
exceeding astonished what would become of the
rest.

" The fire having continued all this night (if I
may call that night which was light as day for ten
miles round about, after a dreadful manner),
when conspiring with a fierce eastern wind in a very
dry season, I went on foot to the same place ;
and saw the whole south part of the City burning
from Cheapside to the Thames, and all along Cornhill (for it likewise kindled back against the wind
as well as forward), Tower-street, Fenchurch-street,
Gracious-street, and so along to Baynard's Castle,
and was now taking hold of St. Paul's Church,
to which the scaffolds contributed exceedingly.

" The conflagration was so universal, and the

people so astonished, that, from the beginning, I know not by what despondency, or fate, they hardly stirred to quench it ; so that there was nothing heard, or seen, but crying out and lamentation, running about like distracted creatures, without at all attempting to save even their goods ; such a strange consternation there was upon them, so as it burned both in breadth and length, the churches, public halls, Exchange, hospitals, monuments, and ornaments ; leaping after a prodigious manner, from house to house, and street to street, at great distances one from the other. For the heat, with a long set of fair and warm weather, had even ignited the air, and prepared the materials to conceive the fire, which devoured, after an incredible manner, houses, furniture, and every thing.

" Here, we saw the Thames covered with goods floating, all the barges and boats laden with what some had time and courage to save, as, on the other side, the carts, etc., carrying out to the fields, which for many miles were strewed with moveables of all sorts, and tents erecting to shelter both people and what goods they could get away. Oh, the miserable and calamitous spectacle ! such as haply the world had not seen since the foundation of it, nor can be outdone till the universal conflagration thereof. All the sky was of a fiery aspect, like the top of a burning oven, and the light seen above forty miles round-about for many nights. God grant mine eyes may never behold the like, who now saw above 10,000 houses all in one flame ! The noise and cracking and thunder of the impetuous flames, the shrieking of women and children, the hurry of people, the fall of towers, houses, and churches, was like a hideous storm ; and the air all about so hot and inflamed, that at the last one was not able to approach it, so that they were forced to stand still, and let the flames burn on, which they did, for near two miles in length and one in breadth. The clouds also of smoke were dismal, and reached, upon computation, near fifty miles in length. Thus, I left it this afternoon burning, a resemblance of Sodom, or the last day. . . .

"4th. The burning still rages, and it is now gotten as far as the Inner Temple. All Fleet-street, the Old Bailey, Ludgate-hill, Warwick-lane, Newgate, Paul's-chain, Watling-street, now flaming, and most of it reduced to ashes; the stones of Paul's flew like grenados, the melting lead running down the streets in a stream, and the very pavements glowing with fiery redness, so as no horse, nor man, was able to tread on them, and the demolition had stopped all the passages, so that no help could be applied. The eastern wind still more impetuously driving the flames forward. Nothing but the Almighty power of God was able to stop them; for vain was the help of man.

"5th. It crossed towards Whitehall; but oh! the confusion there was then at that Court! It pleased his Majesty to command me, among the rest, to look after the quenching of Fetter-lane end, to preserve (if possible) that part of Holborn, whilst the rest of the gentlemen took their several posts, some at one part, and some at another (for now they began to bestir themselves, and not till now, who hitherto had stood as men intoxicated, with their hands across), and began to consider that nothing was likely to put a stop but the blowing up of so many houses as might make a wider gap than any had yet been made by the ordinary method of pulling them down with engines. This some stout seamen proposed early enough to have saved near the whole City, but this some tenacious and avaricious men, aldermen, &c., would not permit, because their houses must have been of the first. It was, therefore, now commended to be practised ; and my concern being particularly for the hospital of St. Bartholomew, near Smithfield, where I had many wounded and sick men, made me the more diligent to promote it ; nor was my care for the Savoy less.

" It now pleased God, by abating the wind, and by the industry of the people, when almost all was lost infusing a new spirit into them, that the fury of it began sensibly to abate about noon, so as it came no farther than the Temple westward, nor than the entrance of Smithfield, north : but continued all this day and night so impetuous towards Cripplegate and the Tower, as made us all despair. It also brake out again in the Temple ; but the courage of the multitude persisting, and many houses being blown up, such gaps and desolations were soon made, as, with the former three days' consumption, the back fire did not so vehemently urge upon the rest as formerly. There was yet no standing near the burning and glowing ruins by near a furlong's space.

" The coal and wood-wharfs, and magazines of oil, rosin, &c., did infinite mischief, so as the invective which a little before I had dedicated to his Majesty and published, giving warning what probably might be the issue of suffering those shops to be in the City was looked upon as a prophecy.

" The poor inhabitants were dispersed about St.

George's Fields, and Moorfields, as far as Highgate, and several miles in circle, some under tents, some under miserable huts and hovels, many without a rag, or any necessary utensils, bed or board, who from delicateness, riches, and easy accommodations in stately and well-furnished houses, were now reduced to extremest misery and poverty.

" In this calamitous condition, I returned with a sad heart to my house, blessing and adoring the distinguishing mercy of God to me and mine, who, in the midst of all this ruin, was like Lot, in my little Zoar, safe and sound. . . .

" 7th. I went this morning on foot from Whitehall as far as London Bridge, through the late Fleet-street, Ludgate-hill by St. Paul's, Cheapside, Exchange, Bishopsgate, Aldersgate, and out to Moorfields, thence through Cornhill, etc., with extraordinary difficulty, clambering over heaps of yet smoking rubbish, and frequently mistaking where I was : the ground under my feet so hot, that it even burnt the soles of my shoes.

" In the meantime, his Majesty got to the Tower by water, to demolish the houses about the graff, which, being built entirely about it, had they taken fire and attacked the White Tower, where the magazine of powder lay, would undoubtedly not only have beaten down and destroyed all the bridge, but sunk and torn the vessels in the river, rendered the demolition beyond all expression for several miles about the country.

" At my return, I was infinitely concerned to find that goodly church, St. Paul's, now a sad ruin, and that beautiful portico (for structure comparable to any in Europe, as not long before repaired by

the late King) now rent in pieces, flakes of large
stones split asunder, and nothing remaining entire
but the inscription in the architrave, showing by
whom it was built, which had not one letter of it
defaced ! It was astonishing to see what immense
stones the heat had in a manner calcined, so that
all the ornaments, columns, friezes, capitals, and
projectures of massy Portland stone, flew off, even
to the very roof, where a sheet of lead covering a
great space (no less than six acres by measure) was
totally melted. The ruins of the vaulted roof
falling, broke into St. Faith's, which being filled
with the magazines of books belonging to the
Stationers, and carried thither for safety, they
were all consumed, burning for a week following.
It is also observable that the lead over the altar
at the east end, was untouched, and among the
divers monuments the body of one bishop remained
entire.

" Thus lay in ashes that most venerable church,
one of the most ancient pieces of early piety in the
Christian world, besides near one hundred more.
The lead, iron-work, bells, plate, &c., melted, the
exquisitely wrought Mercers' Chapel, the sumptuous
Exchange, the august fabric of Christ Church, all
the rest of the Companies' Halls, splendid buildings,
arches, entries, all in dust ; the fountains dried up
and ruined, whilst the very waters remained boil-
ing ; the voragos of subterranean cellars, wells, and
dungeons, formerly warehouses, still burning in
stench and dark clouds of smoke ; so that in five
or six miles traversing about I did not see one load
of timber unconsumed, nor many stones but what
were calcined white as snow.

" The people, who now walked about the ruins,

appeared like men in some dismal desert, or rather, in some great city laid waste by a cruel enemy; to which was added the stench that came from some poor creatures' bodies, beds, and other combustible goods. Sir Thomas Gresham's statue, though fallen from its niche in the Royal Exchange, remained entire, when all those of the Kings since the Conquest were broken to pieces. Also the standard in Cornhill, and Queen Elizabeth's effigies, with some arms on Ludgate, continued with but little detriment, whilst the vast iron chains of the City streets, hinges, bars, and gates of prisons, were many of them melted and reduced to cinders by the vehement heat. Nor was I yet able to pass through any of the narrow streets, but kept the widest; the ground and air, smoke and fiery vapour, continued so intense, that my hair was almost singed, and my feet unsufferably surbated. The bye-lanes and narrow streets were quite filled up with rubbish; nor could one have possibly known where he was, but by the ruins of some Church, or Hall, that had some remarkable tower, or pinnacle remaining.

"I then went towards Islington and Highgate, where one might have seen 200,000 people of all ranks and degrees dispersed, and lying along by their heaps of what they could save from the fire, deploring their loss; and, though ready to perish for hunger and destitution, yet not asking one penny for relief, which to me appeared a stranger sight than any I had yet beheld. His Majesty and Council indeed took all imaginable care for their relief, by proclamation for the country to come in and refresh them with provisions."

Parliament.

While the monarchy was losing ground, another factor in the Government was consolidating itself. This was Parliament. Apparently restored in 1660 to its old position with the Lords back again with the pomp of former days, Parliament was really much stronger than under the early Stuarts. Despite corruption, it could control the King by appropriating his supplies for certain purposes, and by auditing his accounts ; it could attack the King through his ministers. Pepys was shrewd enough to see this trend of events and it is to him rather than to Evelyn that we must look for enlightenment :

" This day, I hear, the Parliament have ordered a bill to be brought in for restoring the Bishops to the House of Lords ; which they had not done so soon but to spite Mr. Prin, who is every day so bitter against them in his discourse in the House." [Pepys, *30th May*, 1661.]

" I went to Westminster, where in the House of Lords I saw his Majesty sit on his throne, but without his robes, all the peers sitting with their hats on ; the business of the day being the divorce of my Lord Ross. Such an occasion and sight had not been seen in England since the time of Henry VIII." [Evelyn, *22nd March*, 1670.]

" After dinner comes Sir Fr. Hollis to me about business ; and I with him by coach to the Temple, and there I 'light ; all the way he telling me romantic lies of himself and his family, how they have been Parliament-men for Grimsby, he and his fore-fathers, this 140 years ; and his father is now : and himself, at this day, stands for to be, with his father, by the death of his fellow-burgess ; and

that he believes it will cost him as much as it did
his predecessor, which was £300 in ale, and £52 in
buttered ale ; which I believe is one of his devilish
lies." [Pepys, 28th September, 1667.]

" The Parliament, it seems, have voted the King
£1,250,000 at £50,000 per month tax for the war ;
and voted to assist the King against the Dutch, and
all that shall adhere to them." [Pepys, 16th
October, 1665.]

" The great Proviso passed the House of Parliament yesterday ; which makes the King and Court
mad, the King having given order to my Lord Chamberlain to send to the playhouses and brothels, to
bid all the Parliament-men that were there to go
to the Parliament presently. This is true, it seems ;
but it was carried against the Court by thirty or forty
voices. It is a Proviso to the Poll Bill, that there
shall be a Committee of nine persons that shall have
the inspection upon oath, and power of giving others,
of all the accounts of the money given and spent
for this war." [Pepys, 8th December, 1666.]

" They did here in the House talk boldly of the
King's bad counsellors, and how they all must
be turned out, and many others, and better brought
in. [Pepys, 17th February, 1668.]

" Then by water from the Privy-stairs to Westminster Hall ; and, taking water, the King and the
Duke of York were in the new buildings ; and the
Duke of York called to me whither I was going ?
and I answered aloud, ' To wait on our masters at
Westminster ; ' at which he and all the company
laughed ; but I was sorry and troubled for it
afterwards, for fear any Parliament-man should
have been there ; and it will be a caution to me for
the time to come." [Pepys, 22nd April, 1668.]

The Protestant Revolution of 1688.

This attack on the Monarchy culminated in 1688. Both Charles II. and James II. were trying to make themselves stronger and to do something for their religion, Roman Catholicism. Foreign aid was invoked, Louis XIV. by the Secret Treaty of Dover, 1670, promising money and troops. This was the real Popish Plot which so alarmed the nation. What is called the Popish Plot occurred in 1678 and 1679 and was merely a scare. The real Popish Plot led the English to try to exclude Charles's Roman Catholic brother, James, from the throne, a policy which failed in 1681, and succeeded in 1688. It is Evelyn who tells this story :

" A few days before this, the Treasurer of the Household, Sir Thomas Clifford, hinted to me, as a confidant, that his Majesty would *shut up the Exchequer* (and, accordingly, his Majesty made use of infinite treasure there, to prepare for an intended rupture) ; but, says he, it will soon be open again, and everybody satisfied ; for this bold man, who had been the sole adviser of the King to invade that sacred stock (though some pretend it was Lord Ashley's counsel, then Chancellor of the Exchequer), was so over-confident of the success of this unworthy design against the Smyrna merchants, as to put his Majesty on an action which not only lost the hearts of his subjects, and ruined many widows and orphans, whose stocks were lent him, but the reputation of his Exchequer for ever, it being before in such credit, that he might have commanded half the wealth of the nation.

" The credit of this bank being thus broken, did exceedingly discontent the people, and never did his Majesty's affairs prosper to any purpose after it,

for as it did not supply the expense of the medi-
tated war, so it melted away, I know not how.

" To this succeeded the King's Declaration for
an universal toleration ; Papists, and swarms
of Sectaries, now boldly showing themselves in their
public meetings. This was imputed to the same
council, Clifford warping to Rome as was believed,
nor was Lord Arlington clear of suspicion, to gratify
that party, but as since it has proved, and was then
evidently foreseen, to the extreme weakening the
Church of England and its Episcopal Government,
as it was projected. I speak not this as my own
sense, but what was the discourse and thoughts of
others, who were lookers-on ; for I think there
might be some relaxations without the least prejudice to the present Establishment, discreetly
limited, but to let go the reins in this manner, and
then to imagine they could take them up again as
easily, was a false policy, and greatly destructive.
The truth is, our Bishops slipped the occasion ;
for, had they held a steady hand upon his Majesty's
restoration, as they might easily have done, the
Church of England had emerged and flourished,
without interruption ; but they were then remiss,
and covetous after advantages of another kind,
whilst his Majesty suffered them to come into a
harvest, with which, without any injustice, he
might have remunerated innumerable gallant
gentlemen for their services, who had ruined themselves in the late rebellion. [1672.]

" The Parliament and the whole Nation were
alarmed about a conspiracy of some eminent
Papists for the destruction of the King and introduction of Popery, discovered by one Oates and
Dr. Tongue, *which last I knew, being the translator*

of the ' Jesuits' Morals ' ; I went to see and con-
verse with him at Whitehall, with Mr. Oates, one
that was lately an apostate to the Church of Rome,
and now returned again with this discovery. He
seemed to be a bold man, and, in my thoughts,
furiously indiscreet ; but everybody believed what
he said ; and it quite changed the genius and
motions of the Parliament, growing now corrupt
and interested with long sitting and court practices ;
but, with all this, Popery would not go down. This
discovery turned them all as one man against it,
and nothing was done but to find out the depth of
this. Oates was encouraged, and everything he
affirmed taken for gospel ;—the truth is, the Roman
Catholics were exceeding bold and busy everywhere,
since the Duke forbore to go any longer to the
chapel. [1st October, 1678.]

" 21st. The murder of Sir Edmondbury Godfrey,
found strangled about this time, as was manifest,
by the Papists, he being the Justice of the Peace,
and one who knew much of their practices, as
conversant with Coleman (a servant of the . . . .
now accused), put the whole nation into a new
ferment against them.

" 15th. The Queen's birthday. I never saw the
Court more brave, nor the nation in more apprehension and consternation. Coleman and one
Staly had now been tried, condemned, and executed. On this, Oates grew so presumptuous, as
to accuse the Queen of intending to poison the
King ; which certainly that pious and virtuous
lady abhorred the thoughts of, and Oates's circumstances made it utterly unlikely in my opinoin.
He probably thought to gratify some who would
have been glad his Majesty should have married

a fruitful lady ; but the King was too kind a husband to let any of these make impression on him. However, divers of the Popish peers were sent to the Tower, accused by Oates ; and all the Roman Catholic lords were by a new Act for ever excluded the Parliament ; which was a mighty blow. The King's, Queen's, and Duke's servants, were banished, and a test to be taken by everybody who pretended to enjoy any office of public trust, and who would not be suspected of Popery. [15*th November*, 1678.]

" 18*th*. I went early to the Old Bailey Sessions-house, to the famous trial of Sir George Wakeman, one of the Queen's physicians, and three Benedictine monks ; the first (whom I was well acquainted with, and take to be a worthy gentleman abhorring such a fact) for intending to poison the King ; the others as accomplices to carry on the plot, to subvert the government, and introduce Popery. The Bench was crowded with the Judges, Lord Mayor, Justices, and innumerable spectators. The chief accusers, Dr. Oates (as he called himself), and one Bedlow, a man of inferior note. Their testimonies were not so pregnant, and I fear much of it from hearsay, but swearing positively to some particulars, which drew suspicion upon their truth ; nor did circumstances so agree, as to give either the Bench, or Jury, so entire satisfaction as was expected. After, therefore, a long and tedious trial of nine hours, the Jury brought them in not guilty, to the extraordinary triumph of the Papists, and without sufficient disadvantage and reflections on witnesses, especially Oates and Bedlow.

" This was a happy day for the Lords in the Tower, who expecting their trial, had this gone

4

against the prisoners at the bar, would all have been in the utmost hazard. For my part, I look on Oates as a vain, insolent man, puffed up with the favour of the Commons for having discovered something really true, more especially as detecting the dangerous intrigue of Coleman, proved out of his own letters, and of a general design which the Jesuited party of the Papists ever had and still have, to ruin the Church of England ; but that he was trusted with those great secrets he pretended, or had any solid ground for what he accused divers noblemen of, I have many reasons to induce my contrary belief. That among so many commissions as he affirmed to have delivered to them from P. Oliva and the Pope,—he who made no scruple of opening all other papers, letters, and secrets, should not only not open any of those pretended commissions, but not so much as take any copy or witness of any one of them, is almost miraculous. But the Commons (some leading persons I mean of them) had so exalted him, that they took all he said for gospel, and without more ado ruined all whom he named to be conspirators ; nor did he spare whoever came in his way. But indeed the murder of Sir Edmundbury Godfrey, suspected to have been compassed by the Jesuits' party for his intimacy with Coleman (a busy person whom I also knew), and the fear they had that he was able to have discovered things to their prejudice, did so exasperate not only the Commons but all the nation, that much of these sharpnesses against the more honest Roman Catholics who lived peaceably, is to be imputed to that horrid fact.

" The sessions ended, I dined or rather supped (so late it was) with the Judges in the large room annexed to the place, and so returned home. Though it was not my custom or delight to be often present at any capital trials, we having them commonly so exactly published by those who take them in short-hand, yet I was inclined to be at this signal one, that by the ocular view of the carriages and other circumstances of the managers and parties concerned, I might inform myself, and regulate my opinion of a cause that had so alarmed the whole nation." [18th July, 1679.]

Of the trial of one of the last victims of the Popish Plot, Lord Stafford, Evelyn has given a long account : " 6th. Sir William Jones summoned up the evidence ; to him succeeded all the rest of the managers, and then Mr. Henry Poule made a vehement oration. After this my Lord, as on all occasions, and often during the trial, spoke in his own defence, denying the charge altogether, and that he had never seen Oates, or Turberville, at the time and manner affirmed : in truth, their testimony did little weigh with me ; Dugdale's only seemed to press hardest, to which my Lord spake a great while, but confusedly, without any method.

" One thing my Lord said as to Oates, which I confess did exceedingly affect me ; That a person who during his depositions should so vauntingly brag that though he went over to the Church of Rome, yet he was never a Papist, nor of their religion, all the time that he seemed to apostatise from the Protestant, but only as a spy ; though he confessed he took their sacrament, worshipped images, went through all their oaths, and discipline of their proselytes, swearing secrecy and to be faithful, but with intent to come over again and betray them ;—that such an hypocrite, that had so deeply prevaricated as even to turn idolater (for so we of the Church of England termed it), attesting God so solemnly that he was entirely theirs and devoted to their interest, and consequently (as he pretended) trusted;—I say, that the witness of such a profligate wretch should be admitted against the life of a peer,—this my Lord looked upon as a monstrous thing, and such as must needs redound to the dishonour of our religion and nation. And verily I am of his Lordship's opinion; such a man's testimony should not be taken against the life of a dog. But the merit of something material which he discovered against Coleman, put him in such esteem with the Parliament, that now, I fancy, he stuck at nothing, and thought everybody was to take what he said for gospel.

"The consideration of this, and some other circumstances, began to stagger me; particularly how it was possible that one who went among the Papists on such a design, and pretended to be intrusted with so many letters and commissions from the Pope and the party, nay and delivered them to so many great persons, should not reserve one of them to show, nor so much as one copy of any commission, which he who had such dexterity in opening letters might certainly have done, to the undeniable conviction of those whom he accused; but, as I said, he gained credit on Coleman. But, as to others whom he so madly flew upon, I am little inclined to believe his testimony, he being so slight a person, so passionate, ill-bred, and of such impudent behaviour; nor is it likely that such piercing politicians as the Jesuits should trust him with so high and so dangerous secrets."
[*6th October*, 1680.]

As a counter stroke came a Protestant Plot:
" *28th*. After the Popish Plot, there was now
a new and (as they called it) a Protestant Plot
discovered, that certain Lords and others should
design the assassination of the King and the Duke
as they were to come from Newmarket, with a
general rising of the nation, and especially of the
City of London, disaffected to the present Government. Upon which were committed to the Tower,
the Lord Russell, eldest son of the Earl of Bedford,
the Earl of Essex, Mr. Algernon Sidney, son to the
old Earl of Leicester, Mr. Trenchard, Hampden,
Lord Howard of Escrick, and others. A proclamation was issued against my Lord Grey, the Duke
of Monmouth, Sir Thomas Armstrong, and one
Ferguson, who had escaped beyond sea ; of these
some were said to be for killing the King, others for
only seizing on him, and persuading him to new
counsels, on the pretence of the danger of Popery,
should the Duke live to succeed, who was now
again admitted to the councils and cabinet secrets.
The Lords Essex and Russell were much deplored,
for believing they had any evil intention against
the King, or the Church ; some thought they were
cunningly drawn in by their enemies for not
approving some late counsels and management
relating to France, to Popery, to the persecution
of the Dissenters, &c. They were discovered by
the Lord Howard of Escrick and some false brethren of the club, and the design happily broken ;
had it taken effect, it would, to all appearance,
have exposed the Government to unknown and
dangerous events ; which God avert ! "

The death of Charles II. produced a lull: " *4th
February*. I went to London, hearing his Majesty

had been the Monday before (2nd February) surprised in his bed-chamber with an apoplectic fit, so that if, by God's providence, Dr. King (that excellent chirurgeon as well as physician) had not been accidentally present to let him blood (having his lancet in his pocket), his Majesty had certainly died that moment; which might have been of direful consequence, there being nobody else present with the King save this Doctor and one more, as I am assured. It was a mark of the extraordinary dexterity, resolution, and presence of mind in the Doctor, to let him blood in the very paroxysm, without staying the coming of other physicians, which regularly should have been done, and for want of which he must have a regular pardon, as they tell me.

" This rescued his Majesty for the instant, but it was only a short reprieve. He still complained, and was relapsing, often fainting, with sometimes epileptic symptoms, till Wednesday, for which he was cupped, let blood in both jugulars, and both vomit and purges, which so relieved him, that on Thursday hopes of recovery were signified in the public Gazette, but that day about noon, the physicians thought him feverish. This they seemed glad of, as being more easily allayed and methodically dealt with than his former fits; so as they prescribed the famous Jesuit's powder; but it made him worse, and some very able doctors who were present did not think it a fever, but the effect of his frequent bleeding and other sharp operations used by them about his head, so that probably the powder might stop the circulation, and renew his former fits, which now made him very weak.

" Thus he passed Thursday night with great

difficulty, when complaining of a pain in his side, they drew twelve ounces more of blood from him ; this was by six in the morning on Friday, and it gave him relief, but it did not continue, for being now in much pain, and struggling for breath, he lay dozing, and, after some conflicts, the physicians despairing of him, he gave up the ghost at half an hour after eleven in the morning, being the sixth of February, 1685, in the 36th year of his reign, and 54th of his age.

" Prayers were solemnly made in all the churches, especially in both the Court Chapels, where the chaplains relieved one another every half quarter of an hour from the time he began to be in danger till he expired, according to the form prescribed in the Church-offices. Those who assisted his Majesty's devotions were, the Archbishop of Canterbury, the Bishops of London, Durham, and Ely, but more especially Dr. Ken, the Bishop of Bath and Wells. It is said they exceedingly urged the receiving Holy Sacrament, but his Majesty told them he would consider of it, which he did so long till it was too late. Others whispered that the Bishops and Lords, except the Earls of Bath and Feversham, being ordered to withdraw the night before, Huddleston, the priest, had presumed to administer the Popish offices.

" He gave his breeches and keys to the Duke, who was almost continually kneeling by his bed side, and in tears. He also recommended to him the care of his natural children, all except the Duke of Monmouth, now in Holland, and in his displeasure. He entreated the Queen to pardon him (not without cause) ; who a little before had sent a bishop to excuse her not more frequently visiting him, in regard of her excessive grief, and withal that his Majesty would forgive it if at any time she had offended him. He spake to the Duke to be kind to the Duchess of Cleveland, and especially Portsmouth, and that Nelly might not starve.

"Thus died King Charles II., of a vigorous and robust constitution, and in all appearance promising a long life. He was a prince of many virtues, and many great imperfections; debonaire, easy of access, not bloody nor cruel; his countenance fierce, his voice great, proper of person, every motion became him; a lover of the sea, and skilful in shipping; not affecting other studies, yet he had a laboratory, and knew of many empirical medicines, and the easier mechanical mathematics; he loved planting and building, and brought in a politer way of living, which passed to luxury and intolerable expense. He had a particular talent in telling a story, and facetious passages, of which he had innumerable; this made some buffoons and vicious wretches too presumptuous and familiar, not worthy the favour they abused. He took delight in having a number of little spaniels follow him and lie in his bed-chamber, where he often suffered the bitches to puppy and give suck, which rendered it very offensive, and indeed made the whole court nasty and stinking. He would doubtless have been an excellent prince, had he been less addicted to women, who made him uneasy, and always in want to supply their unmeasurable profusion, to the detriment of many indigent persons who had signally served both him and his father. He frequently and easily changed favourites to his great prejudice.

" As to other public transactions, and unhappy miscarriages, 'tis not here I intend to number them ; but certainly never had King more glorious opportunities to have made himself, his people, and all Europe happy, and prevented innumerable mischiefs, had not his too easy nature resigned him to be managed by crafty men, and some abandoned and profane wretches who corrupted his otherwise sufficient parts, disciplined as he had been by many afflictions during his banishment, which gave him much experience and knowledge of men and things ; but those wicked creatures took him from off all application becoming so great a King. The history of his reign will certainly be the most wonderful for the variety of matter and accidents, above any extant in former ages : the sad tragical death of his father, his banishment and hardships, his miraculous restoration, conspiracies against him, parliaments, wars, plagues, fires, comets, revolutions abroad happening in his time, with a thousand other particulars. He was ever kind to me, and very gracious upon all occasions, and therefore I cannot without ingratitude but deplore his loss, which for many respects, as well as duty, I do with all my soul." [Evelyn, *4th February*, 1685.]

The new monarch makes a promise not to challenge the position of the Church of England :

" His Majesty being dead, the Duke, now King James II., went immediately to Council, and before entering into any business, passionately declaring his sorrow, told their Lordships, that since the succession had fallen to him, he would endeavour to follow the example of his predecessor in his clemency and tenderness to his people ; that, however he had been misrepresented as affecting arbitrary power, they should find the contrary; for that the laws of England had made the King as great a monarch as he could desire; that he would endeavour to maintain the Government both in Church and State, as by law established, its principles being so firm for monarchy, and the members of it showing themselves so good and loyal subjects; and that, as he would never depart from the just rights and prerogatives of the Crown, so he would never invade any man's property; but as he had often adventured his life in defence of the nation, so he would still proceed, and preserve it in all its lawful rights and liberties.

" This being the substance of what he said, the Lords desired it might be published, as containing matter of great satisfaction to a jealous people upon this change, which his Majesty consented to. Then were the Council sworn, and a Proclamation ordered to be published that all officers should continue in their stations, that there might be no failure of public justice, till his further pleasure should be known. Then the King rose, the Lords accompanying him to his bedchamber, where, whilst he reposed himself, tired indeed as he was with grief and watching, they returned again into the Council-chamber to take order for the *proclaiming* his Majesty, which (after some debate) they consented should be in the very form his grandfather, King James I., was, after the death of Queen Elizabeth; as likewise that the Lords, &c., should proceed in their coaches through the city for the more solemnity of it. Upon this was I, and several other Gentlemen waiting in the Privy gallery, admitted into the Council-chamber to be witness of what was resolved on.

"Thence with the Lords, the Lord Marshal and Heralds, and other Crown-officers being ready, we first went to Whitehall-gate, where the Lords stood on foot bare-headed, whilst the Herald proclaimed his Majesty's title to the Imperial Crown and succession according to the form, the trumpets and kettle-drums having first sounded three times, which ended with the people's acclamations. Then a herald called the Lords' coaches according to rank, myself accompanying the solemnity in my Lord Cornwallis's coach, first to Temple Bar, where the Lord Mayor and his brethren met us on horseback, in all their formalities, and proclaimed the King ; hence to the Exchange in Cornhill, and so we returned in the order we set forth. Being come to Whitehall, we all went and kissed the King and Queen's hands. He had been on the bed, but was now risen and in his undress. The Queen was in bed in her apartment, but put forth her hand, seeming to be much afflicted, as I believe she was, having deported herself so decently upon all occasions since she came into England, which made her universally beloved." [Evelyn, *4th February*, 1685.]

The way James II. kept or rather did not keep this promise will be seen in the fifth chapter. Hence an invitation was sent to the Protestant, William of Orange, son-in-law of James, to come to free England from tyranny, an invitation which was accepted : " Hourly expectation of the Prince of Orange's invasion heightened to that degree, that his Majesty thought fit to abrogate the Commission for the dispensing Power (but retaining his own right still to dispense with all laws) and restore the ejected Fellows of Magdalen College, Oxford. In the meantime, he called over 5000 Irish, and 4000 Scots, and continued to remove Protestants and put in Papists at Portsmouth and other places of trust, and retained the Jesuits about him, increasing the universal discontent. It brought people to so desperate a pass, that they seemed passionately to long for and desire the landing of that Prince, whom they looked on to be their deliverer from Popish tyranny, praying incessantly for an east wind, which was said to be the only hindrance of his expedition with a numerous army ready to make a descent. To such a strange temper, and unheard-of in former times, was this poor nation reduced, and of which I was an eye-witness. The apprehension was (and with reason) that his Majesty's forces would neither at land nor sea oppose them with that vigour requisite to repel invaders." [7th *October*, 1688.]

"I went to London; heard the news of the Prince having landed at Torbay, coming with a fleet of near 700 sail, passing through the Channel with so favourable a wind, that our navy could not intercept, or molest them. This put the King and Court into great consternation, they were now employed in forming an army to stop their further progress, for they were got into Exeter, and the season and ways very improper for his Majesty's forces to march so great a distance." [5*th November*, 1688.]

"The Prince increases every day in force. Several Lords go in to him. Lord Cornbury carries some regiments, and marches to Honiton, the Prince's headquarters. The City of London in disorder; the rabble pulled down the nunnery newly bought by the Papists of Lord Berkeley, at St. John's. The Queen prepares to go to Portsmouth for safety, to attend the issue of this commotion, which has a dreadful aspect." [14th November, 1688.]

"I saw the King take barge to Gravesend at twelve o'clock—a sad sight! The Prince comes to St. James's, and fills Whitehall with Dutch guards." [18th December, 1688.]

"The great convention being assembled the day before, falling upon the question about the Government, resolved that King James having by the advice of the Jesuits and other wicked persons endeavoured to subvert the laws of Church and State, and deserted the kingdom, carrying away the seals, &c., without any care for the management of the government, had by demise abdicated himself and wholly vacated his right; they did therefore desire the Lords' concurrence to their vote, to place the crown on the next heir, the Prince of Orange, for his life, then to the Princess, his wife, and if she died without issue, to the Princess of Denmark, and she failing, to the heirs of the Prince, excluding for ever all possibility of admitting a Roman Catholic." [15th January, 1689.]

CHAPTER II

THE NATION AT WORK

THIS story, besides giving us a glimpse of England before the Industrial Revolution, also shows the land under a system known as Mercantilism, when the Government controlled the rising industries. Trade was carried on by companies founded under royal protection and the colonies were closely watched so that their goods were a source of profit to the mother country. Pepys's knowledge on this subject is often second-hand and, strange to say, it is to the more aristocratic Evelyn that we turn for our account. It was Evelyn's business instincts—he was a brick maker, etc.—and his selection as a commissioner for trade and plantations (colonies) that directed his interests in this channel.

Both writers have sketches of the various industries so closely watched by the Government : "She (Kate Joyce) tells me how the life-guard, which we thought a little while since was sent down into the country about some insurrection, was sent to Winchcombe, to spoil the tobacco there, which, it seems, the people there do plant contrary to law, and have always done, and still been under force and danger of having it spoiled, as it hath been oftentimes, and yet they will continue to plant it. The place, she says, is a miserable poor place."
[Pepys, 19*th September*, 1667.]

" Here I met Sir G. Downing, who would speak with me, and first to inquire what I paid for my kid's leather gloves I had on my hand, and shewed me others on his, as handsome as this in all points, cost him but 12*d.* a pair, and mine me 2*s.* He told me he had been seven years finding out a man that could dress English sheepskin as it should be—and, indeed, it is now as good, in all respects, as kid, and he says will save £100,000 a year, that goes out to France for kid's skins. Thus he labours very worthily to advance our own trade, but do it with mighty vanity and talking." [Pepys, 8*th September*, 1667.]

" Thence to the Duke of York's playhouse, and there, finding the play begun, we homeward to the Glass-House, and there shewed my cozens the making of glass, and had several things made with great content ; and, among others, I had one or two singing-glasses made, which made an echo to the voice, the first that ever I saw ; but so thin, that the very breath broke one or two of them." [Pepys, 23*rd February*, 1669.]

" Homewards, and took up a boy that had a lanthorne, that was picking up of rags, and got him to light me home, and had great discourse with how he could get sometimes three or four bushells of rags in a day, and got 3*d.* a bushel for them, and many other discourses, what and how many ways there are for poor children to get their livings honestly." [Pepys, 22*nd March*, 1661.]

In the timber trade Pepys is specially interested because of his connection with the Navy : " Commissioner Pett and I being invited, went by Sir John Winter's coach, sent for us, to the Mitre, in Fenchurch Street, to a venison-pasty ; where I

found him a very worthy man ; and good discourse, most of which was concerning the Forest
of Deane, and the timber there, and iron-workes
with their great antiquity, and the vast heap of
cinders which they find, and are now of great
value, being necessary for the making of iron at
this day ; and without which they cannot work :
with the age of many trees there left, at a great
fall in Edward the Third's time, by the name of
forbid-trees, which at this day are called vorbid-
trees." [*Pepys, 14th August, 1662.*]

"About seven o'clock, took horse, and rode
to Bowe, and there staid at the King's Head, and
eat a breakfast of eggs, till Mr. Deane, of Woolwich,
and I rid into Waltham Forest, and there we saw
many trees of the King's a-hewing ; and he showed
me the whole mystery of off-square, wherein the
King is abused in the timber that he buys, which
I shall with much pleasure be able to correct.
We rode to Illford, and there, while dinner was
getting ready, he and I practised measuring of the
tables and other things, till I did understand
measuring of timber and board very well." [*Pepys,
18th August, 1662.*]

Evelyn's wider travels enabled him to see more
of our industrial life : " I went to see the wonderful
engine for weaving silk stockings, said to have been
the invention of an Oxford scholar forty years
since ; and I returned by Fromantil's the famous
clock-maker, to see some pendules, Monsieur
Zulichem being with us." [*3rd May, 1661.*]

" Here, we trifled and bathed, and inter-visited
with the company who frequent the place for
health, till the 30th, and then went to Bristol, a
city emulating London, not for its large extent,

but manner of building, shops, bridge, traffic, exchange, market-place, &c. The governor showed us the castle, of no great concernment. The city wholly mercantile, as standing near the famous Severn, commodiously for Ireland, and the Western world. Here, I first saw the manner of refining sugar and casting it into loaves, where we had a collection of eggs fried in the sugar furnace, together with excellent Spanish wine." [*27th May*, 1654.]

"We arrived at Doncaster, where we lay this night; it is a large fair town, famous for great wax-lights, and good stockings." [*16th August*, 1654.]

"We pass the Humber, an arm of the sea of about two leagues breadth. The weather was bad, but we crossed it in a good barge to Barton, the first town in that part of Lincolnshire. All marsh ground till we came to Brigg, famous for the plantations of licorice, and then had brave pleasant riding to Lincoln, much resembling Salisbury Plain." [*19th August*, 1654.]

"M. Kiviet came to examine whether the soil about the river of Thames would be proper to make clinker-bricks, and to treat with me about some accommodation in order to it." [*2nd December*, 1666.]

"In the mean time they had made an experiment of my receipt of houllies which I mention in my book be made at Maestricht, with a mixture of charcoal dust and loam, and which was tried with success at Gresham College (then being the exchange for the meeting of the merchants since the fire) for everybody to see. . . . Next day, we met again about the fuel at Sir J. Armourer's in the Mews.

" 8*th*. My Lord Brereton and others dined at my house where I showed them proof of my new fuel which was very glowing."

" Then we saw the Haven, seven miles from Harwich. The tide runs out every day, but the bedding being soft mud, it is safe for shipping and a station. The trade of Ipswich is for the most part Newcastle coals, with which they supply London; but it was formerly a clothing town. There is not any beggar asks alms in the whole place, a thing very extraordinary, so ordered by the prudence of the Magistrates. It has in it fourteen or fifteen beautiful churches : in a word, it is for building, cleanness, and good order, one of the best towns in England." [10*th September*, 1677.]

" I went to see my Lord of St. Albans' house, at Byfleet, an old large building. Thence, to the papermills, where I found them making a coarse white paper. They cull the rags which are linen for white paper, woollen for brown ; then they stamp them in troughs to a pap, with pestles, or hammers, like the powder-mills, then put it into a vessel of water, in which they dip a frame closely wired with wire as small as a hair and as close as a weaver's reed ; on this they take up the pap, the superfluous water draining through the wire ; this they dexterously turning, shake out like a pancake on a smooth board between two pieces of flannel, then press it between a great press, the flannel sucking out the moisture ; then, taking it out, they ply and dry it on strings, as they dry linen in the laundry ; then dip it in alum-water, lastly, polish and make it up in quires. They put some gum in the water in which they macerate the rags. The mark we find on the sheets is formed in the wire." [*24th August, 1678.*]

Government control of the workers in these industries—the 'prentices and masters—was also necessary : " He tells me also, how, upon occasion of some 'prentices being put in the pillory to-day, for beating of their masters, or such like thing, in Cheapside, a company of 'prentices come and rescued them, and pulled down the pillory ; and they, being set up again, did the like again. So that the Lord Mayor and Major-General Browne was fain to come and stay there, to keep the peace ; and drums, all up and down the city, was beat to raise the trained bands, for to quiet the town ; and by and by, going out, we saw a trained band stand in Cheapside, on their guard." [Pepys, *26th March,* 1664.]

" To Anthony Joyce's, to our gossip's dinner. I had sent a dozen and half of bottles of wine thither, and paid my double share besides, which is 18*s*. Very merry we were. Great discourse of the fray yesterday in Moorefields, how the butchers at first did beat the weavers, between whom there hath been ever an old competition for mastery, but at last the weavers rallied and beat them. At first, the butchers knocked down all for weavers that had green or blue aprons, till they were fain to pull them off and put them in their breeches. At last, the butchers were fain to pull off their sleeves, that they might not be known, and were soundly beaten out of the field, and some deeply wounded and bruised ; till at last the weavers went out tryumphing, calling £100 for a butcher." [Pepys, *26th July,* 1664.]

Trade, as well as industry, was under government control and was carried on by State-chartered companies : " There was walking in the gallery some of the Barbary company, and there we saw a draught of the armes of the company which the King is of, and so is called the Royale Company." [Pepys, *23rd May*, 1663.]

But it was in controlling our colonies in our own interests that this policy of government control was best seen. It was this policy—the Old Colonial System—which lost us America. Evelyn, as a commissioner for Plantations reveals the aims of the Government : " The Earl of Bristol's house in Queen's Street [Lincoln's Inn Fields] was taken for the Commissioners of Trade and Plantations, and furnished with rich hangings of the King's. It consisted of seven rooms on a floor, with a long gallery, gardens, &c. This day we met the Duke of Buckingham, Earl of Lauderdale, Lord Culpeper, Sir George Carteret, Vice-Chamberlain, and myself, had the oaths given us by the Earl of Sandwich, our President. It was to advise and counsel his Majesty, to the best of our abilities, for the well-governing of his Foreign Plantations, &c., the form very little differing from that given to the Privy Council." [*26th May*, 1671.] . . .

" The first thing we did was, to settle the form of a circular letter to the Governors of all his Majesty's Plantations and Territories in the West Indies and Islands thereof, to give them notice to whom they should apply themselves on all occasions, and to render us an account of their present state and government ; but, what we most insisted on was, to know the condition of New England, which appearing to be very independent

as to their regard to Old England, or His Majesty,
rich and strong as they now were, there were great
debates in what style to write to them ; for the
condition of that Colony was such, that they were
able to contest with all other Plantations about
them, and there was fear of their breaking from
all dependence on this nation ; his Majesty,
therefore, commended this affair more expressly.
We, therefore, thought fit, in the first place, to
acquaint ourselves as well as we could of the state
of that place, by some whom we heard of that
were newly come from thence, and to be informed
of their present posture and condition ; some of
our Council were for sending them a menacing
letter, which those who better understood the
peevish and touchy humour of that Colony, were
utterly against."

" A full appearance at the Council. The matter
in debate was, whether we should send a deputy
to New England, requiring them of the Massa-
chusets to restore such to their limits and respective
possessions, as had petitioned the Council ; this
to be the open commission only ; but, in truth,
with secret instructions to inform us of the condition of those Colonies, and whether they were of
such power, as to be able to resist his Majesty and
declare for themselves as independent of the Crown,
which we were told, and which of late years made
them refractory. Colonel Middleton, being called
in, assured us they might be curbed by a few of
his Majesty's first-rate frigates, to spoil their
trade with the islands ; but, though my Lord
President was not satisfied, the rest were, and we
did resolve to advise his Majesty to send Commissioners with a formal commission for adjusting

boundaries, &c., with some other instructions." [*3rd August*, 1671.]

" At the Council, we entered on enquiries about improving the Plantations by silks, galls, flax, senna, &c., and considered how nutmegs and cinnamon might be obtained, and brought to Jamaica, that soil and climate promising success. Dr. Worsley being called in, spake many considerable things to encourage it. We took order to send to the Plantations, that none of their ships should adventure homeward single, but stay for company and convoys. We also deliberated on some fit person to go as Commissioner to inspect their actions in New England, and, from time to time, report how that people stood affected.—In future, to meet at Whitehall." [*12th March*, 1672.]

CHAPTER III

THE NATION AT ITS STUDIES

Schools.

In the 17th century there were not many schools. Some of the great public schools had been founded and Pepys was fortunate in being a scholar of the famous school of St. Paul's, established by Dean Colet in 1512. The object of the founder was mainly to teach Latin, Greek and the Catechism, for his school, like many of the bigger schools had been brought into line with the Revival of Learning. William Lilly, the first master, wrote a Latin Grammar for use in the school. Evelyn was less fortunate than Pepys in his early education, but he, like Pepys, gives us an insight into school life of the time:

"To Paul's Schoole, it being Opposition-day there. I heard some of their speeches, and they were just as schoolboys used to be, of the seven liberal sciences; but I think not so good as our's were in our time. Thence to Bow Church, to the Court of Arches, where a judge sits, and his proctors about him in their habits, and their pleadings all in Latin. Here I was sworn to give a true answer to my uncle's libells. And back again to Paul's School, and went up to see the head forms posed in Latin, Greek, and Hebrew; but I think they do not answer in any so well as we did, only in geography they did pretty well. Dr. Wilkins and Outram were examiners. So down to the school, where Mr. Crumlum did me much honour by telling many what a present I had made to the school, shewing my Stephanus in four volumes. He also shewed us upon my desire an old edition of the grammer of Colett's, where his epistle to the children is very pretty ; and in rehearsing the creed it is said ' borne of the cleane Virgin Mary.' " [Pepys, *4th February*, 1663.]

" To Paul's School, and up to hear the upper form examined ; and there was kept, by very many of the Mercers, Clutterbucke, Barker, Harrington, and others ; and with great respect used by them all, and had a noble dinner. Here they tell me that, in Dr. Colett's will, he says that he would have a Master found for the School that hath good skill in Latin, and, if it could be, one that had some knowledge of the Greeke ; so little was Greeke known here at that time. Dr. Wilkins and one Mr. Smallwood, Posers." [Pepys, *4th February*, 1664.]

" At Paule's school, where I visited Mr. Crumlum at his house ; and, Lord ! to see how ridiculous a conceited pedagogue he is, though a learned man, he being so dogmaticall in all he do and says. But, among other discourse, we fell to the old discourse of Paule's Schoole ; and he did, upon my declaring my value of it, give me one of Lilly's grammers of a very old impression, as it was in the Catholique times, which I shall much set by." [Pepys, *9th March*, 1665.]

" At Eton I left my wife in the coach, and he and I to the College, and there find all mighty fine. The school good, and the custom pretty of boys cutting their names in the shuts of the window when they go to Cambridge, by which many a one hath lived to see himself a Provost and Fellow, that hath his name in the window standing. To the Hall, and there find the boys' verses, ' De Peste : ' it being their custom to make verses at Shrove-tide. I read several, and very good they were ; better, I think, than ever I made when I was a boy, and in rolls as long and longer than the whole Hall, by much. Here is a picture of Venice hung up, and a monument made of Sir H. Wotton's giving it to the College. Thence to the porter's, in the absence of the butler, and did drink of the College beer, which is very good ; and went into the back fields to see the scholars play." [Pepys, 26th February, 1666.]

Evelyn's education consisted partly of travel, and in his wanderings he notes many interesting things in connection with schools. His account of those famous educationists, and originators of classes, the Jesuits, is exceptionally valuable :

" I visited the Jesuit's School, which for the fame of their method, I greatly desired to see. They were divided into four classes, with several inscriptions over each : as, first, *Ad majorem Dei gloriam ;* over the second, *Princeps diligentiæ ;* the third, *Imperator Byzantiorum ;* over the fourth and uppermost, *Imperator Romanorum.* Under these, the scholars and pupils and their places, or forms with titles and priority according to their proficiency. Their dormitory and lodgings above were exceedingly neat. They have a prison for the offenders and less diligent ; and, in an ample court, to recreate themselves in, is an aviary, and a yard where eagles, vultures, foxes, monkeys, and other animals are kept, to divert the boys withal at their hours of remission. To this school join the music and mathematical schools, and lastly a pretty, neat chapel. The great street is built after the Italian mode, in the middle whereof is erected a glorious crucifix of white and black marble, greater than the life. This is a very fair and noble street, clean, well paved, and sweet to admiration." [Evelyn at Antwerp, 5th October, 1641.]

Of a famous Charity School, Evelyn writes : " I went this evening to see the order of the boys and children at Christ's Hospital. There were near 800 boys and girls so decently clad, cleanly lodged, so wholesomely fed, so admirably taught, some the mathematics, especially the forty of the late King's foundation, that I was delighted to see the progress some little youths of thirteen or fourteen years of age had made. I saw them at supper, visited their dormitories, and much admired the order, economy, and excellent government of this most charitable seminary. Some are taught for the Universities, others designed for seamen, all for trades and callings. The girls are instructed in all such work as becomes their sex and may fit them for good wives, mistresses, and to be a blessing to their generation. They sung a psalm before they sat down to supper in the great Hall, to an organ which played all the time, with such cheerful harmony, that it seemed to me a vision of angels. I came from the place with infinite satisfaction, having never seen a more noble, pious and admirable charity. All these consisted of orphans only. The foundation was of that pious Prince King Edward VI., whose picture (held to be an original of Holbein) is in the court where the Governors meet to consult on the affairs of the Hospital, and his statue in white marble stands in a niche of the wall below, as you go to the church, which is a modern, noble and ample fabric. This foundation has had, and still has, many benefactors." [Evelyn, 10*th March*, 1687.]

Much was expected of a boy in those days. Of the two sons of his patron, Pepys gives a glowing account, but this pales by the side of Evelyn's description of his young son's attainments. This system, however, probably had few permanent results.

" Here I spent alone with my Lady, after dinner, the most of the afternoon, and anon the two twins were sent for from school, at Mr. Taylor's, to come to see me, and I took them into the garden, and there, in one of the summer-houses, did examine them, and do find them so well advanced in their learning, that I am amazed at it : they repeating a whole ode without book out of Horace, and did give me a very good account of any thing almost, and did make me very readily very good Latin, and did give me good account of their Greek grammar, beyond all possible expectation ; and so grave and manly as I never saw, I confess, nor could have believed ; so that they will be fit to go to Cambridge in two years at most." [Pepys, 10*th October*, 1667.]

" After six fits of a quartan agne, with which it pleased God to visit him, died my dear son, Richard, to our inexpressible grief and affliction, five years and three days old only, but at that tender age a prodigy for wit and understanding ; for beauty of body, a very angel ; for endowment of mind, of incredible and rare hopes. To give only a little taste of them, and thereby glory to God, who ' out of the mouths of babes and infants does sometimes perfect his praises,' he had learned all his catechism :

at two years and a half old, he could perfectly read any of the English, Latin, French, or Gothic letters, pronouncing the three first languages exactly. He had, before the fifth year, or in that year, not only skill to read most written hands, but to decline all the nouns, conjugate the verbs regular, and most of the irregular ; learned out ' Puerilis,' got by heart almost the entire vocabulary of Latin and French primitives and words, could make congruous syntax, turn English into Latin, and *vice versâ*, construe and prove what he read, and did the government and use of relatives, verbs, substantives, ellipses, and many figures and tropes, and made a considerable progress in Comenius's *Janua ;* began himself to write legibly, and had a strong passion for Greek. The number of verses he could recite was prodigious, and what he remembered of the parts of plays, which he would also act ; and, when seeing a Plautus in one's hand, he asked what book it was, and, being told it was comedy, and too difficult for him, he wept for sorrow. Strange was his apt and ingenious application of fables and morals ; for he had read Æsop ; he had a wonderful disposition to mathematics, having by heart divers propositions of Euclid that were read to him in play, and he would make lines and demonstrate them. As to his piety, astonishing were his applications of Scripture upon occasion, and his sense of God ; he had learned all his Catechism early, and understood the historical part of the Bible and New Testament to a wonder, how Christ came to redeem mankind, and how, comprehending these necessaries himself, his godfathers were discharged of their promise."
[Evelyn, *27th January*, 1658.]

" I heard and saw such exercises at the election of scholars at Westminster School to be sent to the University in Latin, Greek, Hebrew, and Arabic, in themes and extempory verses, as wonderfully astonished me in such youths, with such readiness and wit, some of them not above twelve or thirteen years of age. Pity it is, that what they attain here so ripely, they either do not retain, or do not improve more considerably when they come to be men, though many of them do ; and no less is to be blamed their odd pronouncing of Latin, so that out of England none were able to understand, or endure it. The examinants, or posers, were Dr. Duport, Greek Professor at Cambridge ; Dr. Fell, Dean of Christ-Church, Oxford ; Dr. Pierson, Dr. Allestree, Dean of Westminster, and any that would." [Evelyn, 13th May, 1661.]

The education of girls was sadly neglected, but here and there a school was to be found. " While I was busy at the Office, my wife sends for me to come home, and what was it but to see the pretty girl which she is taking to wait upon her : and though she seems not altogether so great a beauty as she had before told me, yet indeed she is mighty pretty ; and so pretty, that I find I shall be too much pleased with it, and therefore could be contented as to my judgment, though not to my passion, that she might not come, lest I may be found too much minding her, to the discontent of my wife. She is to come next week. She seems, by her discourse, to be grave beyond her bigness and age, and exceeding well bred as to her deportment, having been a scholar in a school at Bow these seven or eight years." [Pepys, 27th September, 1667.]

" Went to Putney by water, in the barge with divers ladies, to see the Schools, or Colleges, of the young gentlewomen." [Evelyn, *12th May*, 1649.]

Universities.

Although Pepys had great affection for Magdalen College, Cambridge, where he was a sizar in 1651, and to which he bequeathed his wonderful collection of books, yet his descriptions of university life are scanty. Evelyn, on the other hand, is strongly attached to Oxford and would have been very much at home there, at all periods of his life. He has much to say concerning the constitution and methods of the University.

We can well imagine the social diversions having a greater attraction for Pepys : " Up by three o'clock this morning, and rode to Cambridge, and was there by seven o'clock, where, after I was trimmed, I went to Christ College, and found my brother John at eight o'clock in bed, which vexed me. Then to King's College chappel, where I found the scholars in their surplices at the service with the organs, which is a strange sight to what it used in my time to be here. Then with Dr. Fairbrother (whom I met there) to the Rose taverne, and called for some wine, and sent also for Mr. Sanchy, with whom and other gentlemen, friends of his, we were very merry, and I treated them as well as I could, and so at noon took horse, having taken leave of my cozen Angier, and rode to Impington, where I found my old uncle sitting all alone, like a man out of the world : he can hardly see ; but all things else he do pretty livelyly." [Pepys, *15th July*, 1661.]

" The 10th of December my father sent a servant

to bring us necessaries ; and, the plague beginning now to cease, on the 3rd of April, 1637, I left school, where, till about the last year, I have been extremely remiss in my studies ; so as I went to the University rather out of shame of abiding longer at school, than for any fitness, as by sad experience I found : which put me to re-learn all that I had neglected, or but perfunctorily gained.

" 10th May. I was admitted a Fellow-commoner of Baliol College, Oxford ; and, on the 29th, I was matriculated in the vestry of St. Mary's, where I subscribed the Articles, and took the oaths : Dr. Baily, head of St. John's, being vice-chancellor, afterwards bishop. It appears by a letter of my father's, that he was upon treaty with one Mr. Bathurst (afterwards Doctor and President), of Trinity College, who should have been my tutor ; but, lest my brother's tutor, Dr. Hobbs, more zealous in his life than industrious to his pupils, should receive it as an affront and especially for that Fellow-commoners in Baliol were no more exempt from exercise than the meanest scholars there, my father sent me thither to one Mr. George Bradshaw (*nomen invisum !* yet the son of an excellent father, beneficed in Surrey). I ever thought my tutor had parts enough ; but, as his ambition made him much suspected of the College, so his grudge to Dr. Lawrence, the governor of it (whom he afterwards supplanted), took up so much of his time, that he seldom or never had the opportunity to discharge his duty to his scholars. This I perceiving, associated myself with one Mr. James Thicknesse (then a young man of the foundation, afterwards ā Fellow of the house), by whose learned and friendly conversation I received great advantage. At my first arrival, Dr. Parkhurst was master; and, after his decease, Dr. Lawrence, a chaplain of his Majesty's and Margaret Professor, succeeded, an acute and learned person: nor do I much reproach his severity, considering that the extraordinary remissness of discipline had (till his coming) much detracted from the reputation of that College." [Evelyn, 1637.]

"After I was somewhat settled there in my formalities (for then was the University exceedingly regular, under the exact discipline of William Laud, Archbishop of Canterbury, then Chancellor), I added, as benefactor to the library of the College, these books: *Zanchii Opera*, vols, 1, 2, 3; *Granado in Thomam Aquinatem*, vols. 1, 2, 3; *Novarini Electa sacra*, and *Cresolii Anthologia sacra*, authors (it seems) desired by the students of Divinity there." [Evelyn, 10*th May*, 1637.]

" On Monday, I went again to the schools, to hear the several faculties, and in the afternoon tarried out the whole Act in St. Mary's, the long speeches of the Proctors, the Vice-Chancellor, the several Professors, creation of Doctors, by the cap, ring, kiss, &c., those ancient ceremonies and institution being as yet not wholly abolished. Dr. Kendal, now Inceptor amongst others, performing his Act incomparably well, concluded it with an excellent oration, abating his Presbyterian animosities, which he withheld, not even against that learned and pious divine, Dr. Hammond. The Act was closed with the speech of the Vice-Chancellor, there being but four in theology, and three in medicine, which was thought a considerable matter, the times considered. I dined at one Monsieur Fiats, a student of Exeter College, and supped at a magnificent entertainment of Wadham Hall, invited by my dear and excellent friend, Dr. Wilkins, then Warden (after, Bishop of Chester)." [Evelyn, 10th *July*, 1654.]

"In the morning, was celebrated the Encænia of the New Theatre, so magnificently built by the munificence of Dr. Gilbert Sheldon, Archbishop of Canterbury, in which was spent £25,000, as Sir Christopher Wren, the architect (as I remember) told me ; and yet it was never seen by the benefactor, my Lord Archbishop having told me that he never did or ever would see it. It is, in truth, a fabric comparable to any of this kind of former ages, and doubtless exceeding any of the present, as this University does for colleges, libraries, schools, students, and order, all the Universities in the world. To the theatre is added the famous Sheldonian printing-house. This being at the Act and the first time of opening the Theatre (Acts being formerly kept in St. Mary's church, which might be thought indecent, that being a place set apart for the immediate worship of God, and was the inducement for building this noble pile), it was now resolved to keep the present Act in it, and celebrate its dedication with the greatest splendour and formality that might be ; and, therefore, drew a world of strangers, and other company, to the University, from all parts of the nation." [Evelyn, 9th *July*, 1669.]

"10th *July*. The next day began the more solemn lectures in all the faculties, which were performed in the several schools, where all the Inceptor-Doctors did their exercises, the Professors having first ended their reading. The assembly now returned to the Theatre, where the *Terræ filius* (the *University Buffoon*) entertained the auditory with a tedious, abusive, sarcastical rhapsody, most unbecoming the gravity of the University, and that so grossly, that unless it be suppressed, it will be of ill consequence, as I afterwards plainly expressed my sense of it both to the Vice-Chancellor and several Heads of Houses, who were perfectly ashamed of it, and resolved to take care of it in future. The old facetious way of rallying upon the questions was left off, falling wholly upon persons, so that it was rather licentious lying and railing than genuine and noble wit. In my life, I was never witness of so shameful entertainment."

" Having two days before had notice that the University intended me the honour of Doctorship, I was this morning attended by the beadles belonging to the Law, who conducted me to the Theatre, where I found the Duke of Ormond (now Chancellor of the University) with the Earl of Chesterfield and Mr. Spencer (brother to the late Earl of Sunderland). Thence, we marched to the Convocation-House, a convocation having been called on purpose ; here, being all of us robed in the porch, in scarlet with caps and hoods, we were led in by the Professor of Laws, and presented respectively by name, with a short eulogy, to the Vice-Chancellor, who sate in the chair, with all the Doctors and Heads of Houses and masters about the room, which was exceeding full. Then, began the Public Orator his speech, directed chiefly to the Duke of Ormond, the Chancellor ; but in which I had my compliment, in course. This ended, we were called up, and created Doctors according to the form, and seated by the Vice-

Chancellor amongst the Doctors, on his right hand ; then, the Vice-Chancellor made a short speech, and so, saluting our brother Doctors, the pageantry concluded, and the convocation was dissolved. So formal a creation of honorary Doctors had seldom been seen, that a convocation should be called on purpose, and speeches made by the Orator ; but they could do no less, their Chancellor being to receive, or rather do them, this honour. I should have been made Doctor with the rest at the public Act, but their expectation of their Chancellor made them defer it. I was then led with my brother Doctors to an extraordinary entertainment at Doctor Mewes', head of St. John's College, and, after abundance of feasting and compliments, having visited the Vice-Chancellor and other Doctors, and given them thanks for the honour done me, I went towards home the 16th, and got as far as Windsor, and so to my house the next day."

The Royal Society.

Both diarists were keen searchers for knowledge. There were few unusual events and sights which escaped the notice of one or the other. At times Pepys's child-like curiosity and readiness to believe lead to amusing results. Evelyn, on the other hand, has a more scientific mind, but they were both children of the Renaissance for whom everything had its interest.

" I saw in Southwark, at St. Margaret's fair, monkeys and apes dance, and do other feats of activity, on the high rope ; they were gallantly clad *à la monde*, went upright, saluted the company, bowing and pulling off their hats, they saluted one another with as good a grace, as if instructed by a dancing master ; they turned heels over head with a basket having eggs in it, without breaking any ; also, with lighted candles in their hands, and on their heads, without extinguishing them, and with vessels of water without spilling a drop. I also saw an Italian wench dance, and perform all the tricks on the high rope to admiration ; all the court went to see her. Likewise, here was a man who took up a piece of iron cannon of about 400 lb. weight with the hair of his head only." [Evelyn, 13*th September*, 1660.]

" W. Hewer and I went and saw the great tall woman that is to be seen, who is but twenty-one years old, and I do easily stand under her arms." [Pepys, 4*th January*, 1669.]

" To Westminster Hall, where it was full terme. Here all the morning, and at noon to my Lord Crewe's, where one Mr. Templer, an ingenious man and a person of honour he seems to be, dined ; and, discoursing of the nature of serpents, he told us some in the waste places of Lancashire do grow to a great bigness, and do feed upon larkes, which they take thus :—They observe, when the lark is soared to the highest, and do crawl till they come to be just underneath them ; and there they place themselves with their mouth uppermost, and there, as is conceived, they do eject poyson upon the bird ; for the bird do suddenly come down again in its course of a circle, and falls directly into the mouth of the serpent ; which is very strange." [Pepys, 4*th February*, 1662.]

" A large whale was taken betwixt my land abutting on the Thames and Greenwich, which drew an infinite concourse to see it, by water, horse, coach, and on foot, from London, and all parts. It appeared first below Greenwich at low water, for at high water it would have destroyed all the boats, but lying now in shallow water encompassed with boats, after a long conflict, it was killed with a harping iron, struck in the head, out of which spouted blood and water by two tunnels ; and, after a horrid groan, it ran quite on shore, and died. Its length was fifty-eight feet, height sixteen ; black-skinned, like coach-leather ; very small eyes, great tail, only two small fins, a peaked snout, and a mouth so wide, that divers men might have stood upright in it; no teeth, but sucked the slime only as through a grate of that bone which we call whale-bone ; the throat yet so narrow as would not have admitted the least of fishes. The extremes of the cetaceous bones hang downwards from the upper jaw, and are hairy towards the ends and bottom within side : all of it prodigious : but in nothing more wonderful than that an animal of so great a bulk should be nourished only by slime through those grates." [Evelyn, *3rd June*, 1658.]

"Thence, to visit honest and learned Mr. Hartlib, a public spirited and ingenious person, who had propagated many useful things and arts. He told me of the castles which they set for ornament on their stoves in Germany (he himself being a Lithuanian, as I remember), which are furnished with small ordnance of silver on the battlements, out of which they discharge excellent perfumes about the rooms, charging them with a little powder to set them on fire, and disperse the smoke : and, in truth, no more than need, for their stoves are sufficiently nasty. He told me of an ink that would give a dozen copies, moist sheets of paper being pressed on it, and remain perfect ; and a receipt how to take off any print without the least injury to the original. This gentleman was master of innumerable curiosities, and very communicative. I returned home that evening by water, and was afflicted for it with a cold that had almost killed me." [Evelyn, *27th November*, 1655.]

" I went to see Colonel Blount, who showed me the application of the way-wiser to a coach, exactly measuring the miles, and showing them by an index as we went on. It had three circles, one pointing to the number or rods, another to the miles, by 10 to 1000, with all the subdivisions of quarters ; very pretty and useful." [Evelyn, *6th August*, 1657.]

" We tried our Diving-Bell, or engine, in the water-dock at Deptford, in which our curator continued half an hour under water ; it was made of cast lead, let down with a strong cable." [Evelyn, *19th July*, 1661.]

" I tried several experiments on the sensitive plant and humilis, which contracted with the least touch of the sun through a burning-glass, though it rises and opens only when it shines on it." [Evelyn, *9th August*, 1661.]

It is fortunate that a society for promoting knowledge and recording the results of research should arise in these days, the Royal Society, amongst whose first and honoured names were those of our two diarists. At one time Pepys was its President, while Evelyn acted as its Secretary for a period. The latter tells us about its origin :

" I was now chosen (and nominated by his Majesty for one of the Council), by suffrage of the rest of the Members, a Fellow of the Philosophic

Society now meeting at Gresham College, where was an assembly of divers learned gentlemen. This being the first meeting since the King's return ; but it had been begun some years before at Oxford, and was continued with interruption here in London during the Rebellion." [Evelyn, 6th January, 1661.]

The King was keenly interested in the new society and its experiments : " 14th. His Majesty was pleased to discourse with me concerning several particulars relating to our Society, and the planet Saturn, &c., as he sate at supper in the withdrawing-room to his bed-chamber." [Evelyn, 14th May, 1661.]

" This day was read our Petition to his Majesty for his Royal Grant authorizing our Society to meet as a Corporation, with several privileges.' [Evelyn, 8th September, 1661.]

The name was now changed to that of Royal Society : " At the Royal Society, Sir William Petty proposed divers things for the improvement of Shipping ; a versatile keel that should be on hinges, and concerning sheathing ships with thin lead." [Evelyn, 20th November, 1661.]

" I waited on Prince Rupert to our Assembly, where we tried several experiments in Mr. Boyle's *vacuum*. A man thrusting in his arm, upon exhaustion of the air, had his flesh immediately swelled so as the blood was near bursting the veins : he drawing it out, we found it all speckled." [Evelyn, 7th May, 1662.]

" Our Charter being now passed under the broad Seal, constituting us a corporation under the name of the Royal Society for the improvement of natural knowledge by experiment, was this day read, and was all that was done this afternoon, being very large." [Evelyn, *13th August*, 1662.]

" I was admitted and then sworn one of the Council of the Royal Society, being nominated in his Majesty's original grant to be of this Council for the regulation of the Society, and making laws and statutes conducible to its establishment and progress, for which we now set apart every Wednesday morning till they were all finished. Lord Viscount Brouncker (that excellent mathematician) was also by his Majesty, our founder, nominated our first President. The King gave us the arms of England to be borne in a canton in our arms, and sent us a mace of silver gilt, of the same fashion and bigness as those carried before his Majesty, to be borne before our president on meeting days. It was brought by Sir Gilbert Talbot, Master of his Majesty's Jewel-house." [Evelyn, *21st August*, 1662.]

" We now resolved that the Arms of the Society should be a field Argent, with a canton of the arms of England ; the supporters two talbots Argent : crest, an eagle Or holding a shield with the like arms of England, viz., three lions. The words *Nullius in verbâ*. It was presented to his Majesty for his approbation, and orders given to Garter King-at-Arms to pass the diploma of their office for it." [Evelyn, *17th September*, 1662.]

" To our Society, to which his Majesty had sent that wonderful horn of the fish which struck a dangerous hole in the keel of a ship in the India sea, which, being broken off with the violence of the fish, and left in the timber, preserved it from foundering." [Evelyn, *8th June*, 1664.]

" I saw the Royal Society bring their new book,

wherein is nobly writ their charter and laws, and comes to be signed by the Duke as a Fellow; and all the Fellows are to be entered there, and lie as a monument; and the King hath put his, with the word Founder." [Pepys, 9th January, 1665.]

"Thence with Creed to Gresham College, where I had been by Mr. Povy the last week proposed to be admitted a member; and was this day admitted, by signing a book and being taken by the hand of the President, my Lord Brouncker, and some words of admittance said to me. But it is a most acceptable thing to hear their discourse, and see their experiments; which were this day on fire, and how it goes out in a place where the ayre is not free, and sooner out where the ayre is exhausted, which they showed by an engine on purpose." [Pepys, 15th February, 1665.]

"To Gresham College, where Mr. Hooke read a second very curious lecture about the late Comet; among other things, proving very probably that this is the very same Comet that appeared before in the year 1618, and that in such a time probably it will appear again, which is a very new opinion; but all will be in print. Then to the meeting, where Sir G. Carteret's two sons, his own, and Sir N. Slaning, were admitted of the Society: and this day I did pay my admission money, 40s., to the Society. Here was very fine discourses and experiments, but I do lack philosophy enough to understand them, and so cannot remember them. among others, a very particular account of the making of the several sorts of bread in France, which is accounted the best place for bread in the world." [Pepys, 1st March, 1665.]

The activities of the Society were various:
"Anon to Gresham College, where, among other
good discourse, there was tried the great poyson
of Maccassa upon a dogg, but it had no effect all
the time we sat there." [Pepys, *15th March*, 1665.]

"Thence to Gresham College, and there did see
a kitling killed almost quite, but that we could not
quite kill her, with such a way: the ayre out of a
receiver, wherein she was put, and then the ayre
being let in upon her, revives her immediately—
nay, and this is to be made by putting together a
liquor and some body that ferments—the steam
of that do do the work." [Pepys, *22nd March*, 1665.]

"Thence with my Lord Brouncker to Gresham
College, the first time after the sickness that I was
there, and the second time any met. And here a
good lecture of Mr. Hooke's about the trade of
felt-making, very pretty; and anon he alone with
me about the art of drawing pictures by Prince
Rupert's rule and machine, and another of Dr.
Wren's; but he says nothing do like squares, or,
which is the best in the world, like a dark roome."
[Pepys, *21st February*, 1666.]

An interesting experiment in transfusion of
blood was seen: "Dr. Croone told me, that, at
the meeting at Gresham College to-night, which,
it seems, they now have every Wednesday again,
there was a pretty experiment of the blood of one
dog let out, till he died, into the body of another
on one side, while all his own run out on the other
side. The first died upon the place, and the other
very well, and likely to do well. This did give
occasion to many pretty wishes, as of the blood of
a Quaker to be let into an Archbishop, and such
like; but, as Dr. Croone says, may, if it takes,

be of mighty use to man's health, for the mending of bad blood by borrowing from a better body." [*Pepys, 14th November, 1666.*]

"To the Royal Society, which since the sad conflagration were invited by Mr. Howard to sit at Arundel-House in the Strand, who, at my instigation, likewise bestowed on the Society that noble library which his grandfather especially, and his ancestors had collected. This gentleman had so little inclination to books, that it was the preservation of them from embezzlement." [*Evelyn, 9th January, 1667.*]

"After dinner I walked to Arundell House, the way very dusty, the day of meeting of the Society being changed from Wednesday to Thursday, which I knew not before, because the Wednesday is a Council-day, and several of the Council are of the Society, and would come but for their attending the King at Council; where I find very much company, in expectation of the Duchess of New-castle, who had desired to be invited to the Society; and was, after much debate *pro* and *con.*, it seems many being against it; and we do believe the town will be full of ballads of it. Anon comes the Duchess with her women attending her; among others, the Ferabosco, of whom so much talk is that her lady would bid her show her face and kill the gallants. She is indeed black, and hath good black little eyes, but other-wise a very ordinary woman I do think, but they say sings well. The Duchess hath been a good, comely woman; but her dress so antick, and her deportment so ordinary, that I do not like her at all, nor do I hear her say anything that was worth hearing, but that she was full of admiration, all admiration. Several fine experiments were shown her of colours, loadstones, microscopes, and of liquors : among others, of one that did, while she was there, turn a piece of roasted mutton into pure blood, which was very rare. Here was Mrs. Moore of Cambridge, whom I had not seen before, and I was glad to see her ; as also a very black boy that run up and down the room, somebody's child in Arundell House. After they had shown her many experiments, and she cried still she was full of admiration, she departed, being led out and in by several Lords that were there ; among others, Lord George Barkeley and Earl of Carlisle, and a very pretty young man, the Duke of Somerset." [Pepys, 30*th May*, 1667.]

" I read my first discourse *Of Earth and Vegetation* before the Royal Society as a lecture in course, after Sir Robert Southwell had read his the week before *On Water*. I was commanded by our President, and the suffrage of the Society, to print it." [Evelyn, 29*th April*, 1675.]

" Sir Joseph Williamson, Principal Secretary of State, was chosen President of the Royal Society, after my Lord Viscount Brouncker had possessed the chair now sixteen years successively, and therefore now thought fit to *change*, that prescription might not prejudice." [Evelyn, 30*th November*, 1677.]

" The anniversary election at the Royal Society brought me to London, where was chosen President that xcellent person and great philosopher, Mr. Robert Boyle, who indeed ought to have been the very first ; but neither his infirmity nor his modesty could now any longer excuse him. I desired I might for this year be left out of the

Council, by reason my dwelling was in the country.
The Society according to custom dined together."
[Evelyn, 30th November, 1680.]

Newspapers.

Another sign of intellectual life was the publishing of the first English newspapers : "To
Westminster Hall, and there bought the first
newsbooks of L'Estrange's writing, he beginning
this week ; and makes, methinks, but a simple
beginning." [Pepys, 4th September, 1663.]

"Mr. Roger L'Estrange (a gentleman whom I
had long known, and a person of excellent parts,
abating some affectations) appearing first against
the Dissenters in several Tracts, had now for some
years turned his style against those whom (by way
of hateful distinction) they called Whigs and Trim-
mers, under the title of Observator, which came
out three or four days every week, in which sheets,
under pretence to serve the Church of England,
he gave suspicion of gratifying another party, by
several passages which rather kept up animosities
than appeased them, especially now that nobody
gave the least occasion." [Evelyn, 7th May, 1685.]

CHAPTER IV

THE NATION AT PLAY

THE fourth chapter is a somewhat comprehensive one. Though the title suggests amusements, yet more will be given. An attempt will be made to show other aspects of social life, for both diarists have records of the kinds of houses, dress, food, etc., which were then to be met with in these times, records which one would be loath to omit.

Dwellings.

Evelyn in his travels is ever on the alert to visit the homes of the nobles : " I dined at Lord John Berkeley's, newly arrived out of Ireland, where he had been Deputy ; it was in his new house, or rather palace ; for I am assured it stood him in near £30,000. It is very well built, and has many noble rooms, but they are not very convenient, consisting but of one *Corps de Logis ;* they are all rooms of state, without closets. The staircase is of cedar, the furniture is princely : the kitchen and stables are ill-placed, and the corridor worse, having no report to the wings they join to. For the rest, the fore-court is noble, so are the stables ; and, above all, the gardens, which are incomparable by reason of the inequality of the ground, and a pretty piscina. The holly hedges on the terrace I advised the planting of. The porticos are in imitation of a house described by Palladio ; but it happens to be the worst in his book, though my

good friend, Mr. Hugh May, his Lordship's architect, effected it." [Evelyn, *25th September*, 1672.]

"I went to see my Lord Sunderland's Seat at
Althorpe, four miles from the ragged town of
Northampton (since burnt, and well re-built). It
is placed in a pretty open bottom, very finely
watered and flanked with stately woods and groves
in a park, with a canal, but the water is not running,
which is a defect. The house, a kind of modern
building, of freestone, within most nobly furnished ;
the apartments very commodious, a gallery and
noble hall ; but the kitchen being in the body of
the house, and chapel too small, were defects.
There is an old yet honourable gate-house standing
awry, and out-housing mean, but designed to be
taken away. It was moated round, after the old
manner, but it is now dry, and turfed with a beautiful carpet. Above all, are admirable and magnificent the several ample gardens furnished with the
choicest fruit, and exquisitely kept. Great plenty
of oranges, and other curiosities. The park full
of fowl, especially herns, and from it a prospect
to Holmby House, which being demolished in the
late civil wars, shows like a Roman ruin, shaded
by the trees about it, a stately, solemn, and pleasing
view." [Evelyn, *14th July*, 1675.]

Pepys, on the other hand, describes a middle-
class gentleman's house : "And so away for
Huntingdon ; and come to Brampton at about
noon, and there find my father and sister and
brother all well : and up and down to see the
garden with my father, and the house, and do
altogether find it very pretty ; especially the little
parlour and the summer-houses in the garden,
only the wall do want greens upon it, and the

house is too low-roofed ; but that is only because
of my coming from a house with higher ceilings."
[Pepys, 9th October, 1667.]

"This morning my dining-room was finished
with green serge hanging and gilt leather, which
is very handsome." [Pepys, 14th October, 1660.]

Dress.

Men's dress was much more picturesque than
that of the present day, and it was a childish joy
to the self complacent Pepys to make himself
"mighty fine." Evelyn had progressed beyond
such trivialities.

"This night W. Hewer brought me home from
Mr. Pim's my velvet coat and cap, the first that
ever I had. [Pepys, 25th August, 1660.]

"Up, and this day put on my close-kneed
coloured suit, which, with new stockings of the
colour, with belt, and new gilt-handled sword,
is very handsome." [Pepys, 19th April, 1663.]

"To Whitehall on foot, calling at my father's
to change my long black cloak for a short one
(long cloaks being now quite out) ; but he being
gone to church, I could not get one." [Pepys, 17th
October, 1660.]

"I walked to my brother Tom's to see a velvet
cloake, which I buy of Mr. Moore. It will cost me
£8 10s. ; he bought it for £6 10s. ; but it is worth
my money." [Pepys, 17th May, 1662.]

"To Alderman Backwell's, but his servants not
being up, I went home, and put on my grey cloth
suit and faced white coate, made of one of my wife's
pettycoates, the first time I have had it on, and
so in a riding garbe back again." [Pepys, 13th
June, 1661.]

" This morning my brother's man brought me a new black baize waiste-coate, faced with silk, which I put on, from this day laying by half-shirts for this winter. He brought me also my new gown of purple shagg : also, as a gift from my brother, a velvet hat, very fine to ride in, and the fashion, which pleases me." [Pepys, 1st November, 1663.]

A gentleman must possess a beaver hat : " In the evening did bet a bever, an old one, but a very good one, of Sir W. Batten, for which I must give him something ; but I am very well pleased with it." [Pepys, 19th April, 1662.]

So anxious was Pepys to be in the fashion that even his boy had to appear in the newest style : " After dinner, . . . I walked with my wife to my brother Tom's ; our boy waiting on us with his sword, which this day he begins to wear, to outdo Sir W. Pen's boy, who this day, and Sir W. Batten's, do begin to wear new liverys ; but I do take mine to be the neatest of them all. I led my wife to Mrs. Turner's pew, the church being full, it being to hear a Doctor who is to preach a pro-bacon sermon. When Church was done, my wife and I walked to Graye's Inne, to observe fashions of the ladies, because of my wife's making some clothes." [Pepys, 4th May, 1662.]

Wigs began to be worn : " At my periwigg-maker's, and there showed my wife the periwigg made for me, and she likes it very well, and so to my brother's, and to buy a pair of boddice for her." [Pepys, 30th October, 1663.]

" To my great sorrow find myself £43 worse than I was the last month, which was then £760, and now it is but £717. But it hath chiefly arisen from my layings-out in clothes for myself and wife ;

viz., for her about £12, and for myself £55, or
thereabouts ; having made myself a velvet cloak,
two new cloth shirts, black, plain both ; a new
shag gown, trimmed with gold buttons and twist,
with a new hat, and silk tops for my legs, and
many other things, being resolved henceforward
to go like myself. And also two perriwiggs, one
whereof costs me £3, and the other 40s. I have
worn neither yet, but will begin next week, God
willing. I having laid out in clothes for myself,
and wife, and for her closet and other things without, these two months this, and the last, besides
household expenses of victualls, &c., above £110.
But I hope I shall with more comfort labour to
get more, and with better successe than when,
for want of clothes, I was forced to sneak like a
beggar." [Pepys, *31st October, 1663.*]

More unusual still, to us, would be the sight of
a man wearing his wife's muff : " This day I
first did wear a muffe, being my wife's last year's
muffe ; and now I have bought her a new one,
this serves me very well." [Pepys, *30th November,*
1662.]

Pepys also took great care that his pretty wife
should be well dressed : " This the first day that
ever I saw my wife wear black patches since we were
married." [Pepys, *30th August, 1660.*]

" This day my wife put on her black silk gown,
which is now laced all over with black gimp lace,
as the fashion is, in which she is very pretty."
[Pepys, *9th June, 1661.*]

" To church with my wife, who this day put on
her green petticoate of flowred sattin, with fine
white and black gimp lace of her own putting on,
which is very pretty." [Pepys, *29th June, 1662.*]

"Sat late talking with my wife, about our entertaining Dr. Clerke's lady and Mrs. Pierce shortly, being in great pain that my wife hath never a winter gown, being almost ashamed of it that she should be seen in a taffata one, when all the world wears moyre ; but we could not come to any resolution what to do therein, other than to appear as she is." [Pepys, *29th December*, 1662.]

"She [Lady Carteret] tells me the ladies are to go into a new fashion shortly, and that is, to wear short coats above their ancles ; which she and I do not like ; but conclude this long trayne to be mighty graceful." [Pepys, *13th October*, 1666.]

"My wife being dressed this day in fair hair did make me so mad, that I spoke not one word to her, though I was ready to burst with anger. After that, Creed and I into the Park, and walked, a most pleasant evening, and so took coach, and took up my wife, and in my way home discovered my trouble to my wife for her white locks, swearing several times, which I pray God forgive me for, and bending my fist, that I would not endure it. She, poor wretch, was surprized with it, and made me no answer all the way home ; but there we parted, and I to the office late, and then home, and without supper to bed, vexed." [Pepys, *11th May*, 1667.]

Ladies were very " modern " even in those days : " I now observed how the women began to paint themselves, formerly a most ignominious thing." [Evelyn, *11th May*, 1654.]

"Mrs. Pierce is still very pretty, but paints red on her face, which makes me hate her." [Pepys, *26th October*, 1667.]

Charles II. designed a new Court dress which

was never to be changed. It had but a short career.

" This day the King begins to put on his vest, and I did see several persons of the House of Lords and Commons too, great courtiers, who are in it ; being a long cassocke close to the body, of black cloth, and pinked with white silk under it, and a coat over it, and the legs ruffled with black riband like a pigeon's leg : and, upon the whole, I wish the King may keep it, for it is a very fine and handsome garment." [Pepys, 15th October, 1666.]

" The Court is all full of vests, only my Lord St. Albans not pinked, but plain black ; and they say the King says the pinking upon whites makes them look too much like magpies, and, therefore, hath bespoke one of plain velvet." [Pepys, 17th October, 1666.]

Evelyn rejoiced in Charles's innovation, not as Pepys would have done, from personal motives, but because it was a sign of independence in an age when French fashions were slavishly followed : " To court. It being the first time his Majesty put himself solemnly into the eastern fashion of vest, changing doublet, stiff collar, bands and cloak, into a comely vest, after the Persian mode, with girdle or straps, and shoe strings and garters into buckles, of which some were set with precious stones, resolving never to alter it, and to leave the French mode, which had hitherto obtained to our great expense and reproach. Upon which divers courtiers and gentlemen gave his Majesty gold by way of wager that he would not persist in this resolution. I had sometime before presented an invective against that unconstancy, and our so much affecting the French fashion, to his Majesty,

in which I took occasion to describe the comeliness
and usefulness of the Persian clothing, in the very
same manner his Majesty now clad himself. This
pamphlet I intitled 'Tyrannus, or the Mode,'
and gave it to his Majesty to read. I do not impute
to this discourse the change which soon happened,
but it was an identity that I could not but take
notice of." [Evelyn, 30th October, 1666.]

Food.

If we take the epicure, Pepys, as a standard,
the Englishman of his day lived well. Evelyn
apparently considers such mundane affairs as
eating as beneath his notice. But to Pepys these
are amongst the most important functions of life.

" Home from my office to my Lord's lodgings,
where my wife had got ready a very fine dinner—
viz., a dish of marrow-bones ; a leg of mutton ;
a loin of veal ; a dish of fowl, three pullets, and a
dozen of larks all in a dish ; a great tart, a neat's
tongue, a dish of anchovies ; a dish of prawns
and cheese. My company was my father, my uncle
Fenner, his two sons, Mr. Pierce, and all their
wives, and my brother Tom." [Pepys, 20th
January, 1660.]

" My poor wife rose by five o'clock in the morning, before day, and went to market and bought
fowles and many other things for dinner, with
which I was highly pleased, and the chine of
beef was down also before six o'clock, and my
own jacke, of which I was doubtfull, do carry it
very well, things being put in order, and the cook
come. By and by comes Dr. Clerke and his lady,
his sister, and a she-cosen, and Mr. Pierce and his
wife, which was all my guests. I had for them,

after oysters, at first course, a hash of rabbits and lamb, and a rare chine of beef. Next, a great dish of roasted fowle, cost me about 30s., and a tart, and then fruit and cheese. My dinner was noble, and enough. I had my house mighty clean and neat ; my room below with a good fire in it ; my dining-room above, and my chamber being made a withdrawing-chamber ; and my wife's a good fire, also. I find my new table very proper, and will hold nine or ten people well, but eight with great room. At supper, had a good sack posset and cold meat, and sent my guests away about ten o'clock at night, both them and myself highly pleased with our management of this day ; and indeed their company was very fine, and Mrs. Clerke a very witty, fine lady, though a little conceited and proud. I believe this day's feast will cost me near £5." [Pepys, 13th January, 1663.]

With one meal per day, something like the above, Pepys found it advisable to partake sparingly of the other meals : " Mr. Moore and I and another gentleman went out and drank a cup of ale together in the new market, and there I eat some bread and cheese for my dinner." [Pepys, 2nd January, 1660.]

Dishes were washed in a cistern at the table and used again, for the many courses would make a big demand on crockery.

"Up very betimes, and with Jane to Levett's, there to conclude upon our dinner ; and thence to the pewterer's, to buy a pewter sesterne, which I have ever hitherto been without." [Pepys, 14th March, 1668.]

Lest conversation should flag during the lengthy meals, amusement was sometimes provided :

" Dining with my Lady Sunderland, I saw a fellow swallow a knife, and divers great pebble stones, which would make a plain rattling one against another. The knife was in a sheath of horn." [Evelyn, 30th March, 1675.]

At the royal table the custom of tasting the dishes still prevailed : " To White Hall, and saw the King and Queen at dinner ; and observed, which I never did before, the formality, but it is but a formality, of putting a bit of bread wiped upon each dish into the mouth of every man that brings a dish ; but it should be in the sauce." [Pepys, 8th September, 1667.]

Drinks.

In the days before reservoirs, days when tea, coffee and cocoa were rarities, beer was the staple drink. This explains an entry like the following : " I met two little schoolboys going with pichers of ale to their schoolmaster to break up against Easter, and I did drink of some of one of them, and give him two-pence." [Pepys, 11th April, 1661.]

Pepys, however, could afford other drinks : " They both found me under the barber's hands ; but I had a bottle of good sack in the house, and so made them very wellcome." [Pepys, 3rd December, 1660.]

" Being come home, we to cards, till two in the morning, and drinking lamb's-wool. So to bed." [Pepys, 9th November, 1666.]

" I did send for a cup of tee (a China drink) of which I never had drank before." [Pepys, 25th September, 1660.]

" To Creed's chamber, and there sat a good

while and drank chocolate." [Pepys, *17th October*, 1662.]

Evelyn also mentions the custom of drinking chocolate, and has details of how the Moorish ambassadors were in 1682 treated to sherbet. He has also something to say of the origin of coffee drinking : " There came in my tyme to the Coll, one Nathaniel Conopios out of Greece, from Cyrill the Patriarch of Constantinople, who returning many years after, was made (as I understand) Bishop of Smyrna. He was the first I ever saw drink coffee, which custom came not into England till 30 years after." [Evelyn, *10th May*, 1637.]

Mention of coffee brings to mind the famous Wills's Coffee House : " In Covent Garden to-night, going to fetch home my wife, I stopped at the great Coffee-house there, where I never was before : where Dryden, the poet, I knew at Cambridge, and all the wits of the town, and Harris the player, and Mr. Hoole, of our College. And, had I had time then, or could at other times, it will be good coming thither, for there, I perceive, is very witty and pleasant discourse. But I could not tarry, and, as it was late, they were all ready to go away." [Pepys, *3rd February*, 1664.]

Pepys could find time, however, to become acquainted with the taverns. He visits the Fleece to drink " mum " (a species of beer), the Dog, the Three Cranes, the Mitre, the Sun and a host of others. On May 10th, 1663, he is seen partaking of the " ordinary " at the King's Head : " After that to some other discourse, and, among other things, talking of the way of Ordinaries, that it is very convenient, because a man knows what he hath to pay : one did wish that, among many bad, we

could learn her good things, of France, which
were that we would not think it below the gentleman, or person of honour, at a taverne, to bargain
for his meat before he eats it ; and next, to take
his servants without certificate from some friend
or gentleman of his good behaviour and abilities."

Domestic Amusements.

There was no lack of domestic amusements
though, as one might expect, betting was too closely
connected with many of them.

Card playing was fashionable and Pepys naïvely
confesses his ventures : " Going and coming,
we played at gleeke, and I won 9s. 6d. clear, the
most that ever I won in my life. I pray God it
may not tempt me to play again." [Pepys, 17th
February, 1662.]

" He told me my Lord do begin to settle (to)
business again and that the King did send for
him the other day to my Lady Castlemaine's, to
play at cards, where he lost £50 ; for which I am
sorry, though he says my Lord was pleased at it,
and said he would be glad at any time to lose £50 for
the King to send for him to play, which I do not
so well like." [Pepys, 14th May, 1663.]

Betting was also associated with backgammon
and billiards : " Thence, after losing a crowne
betting at Tables, we walked home, Cocke seeing
me to my new lodging." [Pepys, 21st September,
1665.]

" After dinner, beat Captain Cocke at billiards ;
won about 8s. of him and my Lord Brouncker."
[Pepys, 14th August, 1665.]

Evelyn describes a new kind of billiard table
at the home of Charles II.'s favourite, Lady Cleve-

land : " There was a billiard-table, with as many more hazards as ours commonly have ; the game being only to prosecute the ball till hazarded, without passing the port, or touching the pin ; if one miss hitting the ball every time, the game is lost, or if hazarded. It is more difficult to hazard a ball, though so many, than in our table, by reason the bound is made so exactly even, and the edges not stuffed ; the balls are also bigger, and they for the most part use the sharp and small end of the billiard-stick, which is shod with brass, or silver." [Evelyn, 4th December, 1679.]

Pepys disapproves of open gaming but his curiosity is too great for him to miss seeing what it is like : " To my Lord Sandwich's, whom I find missing his ague fit to-day, and is pretty well, playing at dice, and by this I see how time and example may alter a man ; he being now acquainted with all sorts of pleasures and vanities, which heretofore he never thought of, nor loved, nor, it may be, hath allowed, with Ned Pickering and his page Lond." [Pepys, 28th January, 1663.]

" By and by I met with Mr. Brisband ; and having it in my mind this Christmas to do what I never can remember that I did, go to see the gaming at the Groome-Porter's, I having in my coming from the playhouse stepped into the two Temple-halls, and there saw the dirty 'prentices and idle people playing ; wherein I was mistaken, in thinking to have seen gentlemen of quality playing there, as I think it was when I was a little child, that one of my father's servants, John Bassum, I think, carried me in his arms thither. I did tell Brisband of it, and he did lead me thither, where, after staying an hour, they begun to play at about eight at night, where to see how differently one man took his losing from another, one cursing and swearing, and another only muttering and grumbling to himself, a third without any apparent discontent at all : to see how the dice will run good luck in one hand, for half an hour together, and another have no good luck at all : to see how easily here, where they play nothing but guinnys, a £100 is won or lost : to see two or three gentlemen come in there drunk, and putting their stock of gold together, one 22 pieces, the second 4, and the third 5 pieces ; and these two play one with another, and forget how much each of them brought, but he that brought the 22 thinks that he brought no more than the rest : to see the different humours of gamesters to change their luck, when it is bad, how ceremonious they are to call for new dice, to shift their places, to alter their manner of throwing and that with great industry, as if there was anything in it : to see how some old gamesters, that have no money now to spend as formerly, do come and sit and look on, and among others, Sir Lewes Dives, who was here, and hath been a great gamester in his time : to hear their cursing and damning to no purpose, as one man being to throw a seven if he could, and, failing to do it after a great many throws, cried he would be damned if ever he flung seven more while he lived, his despair of throwing it being so great, while others did it as their luck served almost every throw : to see how persons of the best quality do here sit down, and play with people of any, though meaner ; and to see how people in ordinary clothes shall come hither and play away 100, or 2 or 300 guinnys, without any kind of difficulty : and lastly, to see the formality

of the groome-porter, who is their judge of all
disputes in play and all quarrels that may arise
therein, and how his under-officers are there to
observe true play at each table, and to give new
dice, is a consideration I never could have thought
had been in the world, had I not now seen it. And
mighty glad I am that I did see it, and it may be
will find another evening, before Christmas be
over, to see it again, when I may stay later, for
their heat of play begins not till about eleven or
twelve o'clock ; which did give me another pretty
observation of a man, that did win mighty fast
when I was there. I think he won £100 at single
pieces in a little time. While all the rest envied
him his good fortune he cursed it, saying, " it
come so early upon me, for this fortune two hours
hence would be worth something to me, but then
I shall have no such luck.' This kind of prophane,
mad entertainment they give themselves. And
so I, having enough for once, refusing to venture,
though Brisband pressed me hard, and tempted
me with saying that no man was ever known to
lose the first time, the devil being too cunning to
discourage a gamester ; and he offered me also
to lend me ten pieces to venture ; but I did refuse,
and so went away." [Pepys, 1st *January*, 1668.]

Turning to a pleasanter side we find simple
diversions such as blindman's buff, drawing and
dancing : " To Sir W. Batten's, where Mr. Coventry
and all our families here, and Sir R. Ford and his,
and a great feast, and good discourse and merry,
and so home to bed, where my wife and people
innocently at cards, very merry. I to bed, leaving,
them to their sport and blindman's buff." [Pepys,
26th *December*, 1664.]

" Up, and to church with my wife. Yesterday begun my wife to learn to limn of one Browne, which Mr. Hill helps her to, and by her beginning, upon some eyes, I think, she will do very fine things, and I shall take great delight in it." [Pepys, *7th May*, 1665.]

" Mr. Povy and I to White Hall ; he taking me thither on purpose to carry me into the ball this night before the King. He brought me first to the Duke's chamber, where I saw him and the Duchess at supper ; and thence into the room where the ball was to be, crammed with fine ladies, the greatest of the Court. By and by, comes the King and Queen, the Duke and Duchess, and all the great ones : and after seating themselves, the King takes out the Duchess of York ; and the Duke, the Duchess of Buckingham ; the Duke of Monmouth, my Lady Castlemaine ; and so other lords other ladies : and they danced the Brantle. After that, the King led a lady a single Coranto ; and then the rest of the lords, one after another, other ladies : very noble it was, and great pleasure to see. Then to country dances ; the King leading the first, which he called for ; which was, says he, ' Cuckolds all awry,' the old dance of England. Of the ladies that danced, the Duke of Monmouth's mistress, and my Lady Castlemaine, and a daughter of Sir Harry de Vicke's, were the best. The manner was, when the King dances, all the ladies in the room, and the Queen herself, stand up ; and indeed he dances rarely, and much better than the Duke of York. Having staid here as long as I thought fit, to my infinite content, it being the greatest pleasure I could wish now to see at Court, I went home, leaving them dancing." [Pepys, *31st December*, 1662.]

"The dancing-master [Pembleton] come, whom standing by, seeing him instructing my wife, when he had done with her, he would needs have me try the steps of a coranto ; and what with his desire and my wife's importunity, I did begin, and then was obliged to give him entry money 10s., and am become his scholler. The truth is, I think it is a thing very useful for any gentleman." [Pepys, 4th May, 1663.]

But Pepys's chief delight was in music. Master of several instruments, vocalist and composer, he is able to speak with authority about most aspects of music. We read of many instruments—the flageolet, lute, viol, guitar, harpsichord, spinet, recorder, trumpet marine, dulcimer, theorbo, and even of drums, triangle, and bagpipes.

"At night to my viallin (the first time that I have played on it since I come to this house) in my dining-roome, and afterwards to my lute there, and I took much pleasure to have the neighbours come forth into the yard to hear me." [Pepys, 21st November, 1660.]

"In my way, in Leadenhall Street, there was morris-dancing, which I have not seen a great while. So set up my horse at Games's, paying 5s. for him, and went to hear Mrs. Turner's daughter play on the harpsichon ; but, Lord ! it was enough to make any one sick to hear her ; yet was I forced to commend her highly." [Pepys, 1st May, 1663.]

"With Lord Brouncker to the Duke of York's playhouse, where we saw 'The Unfortunate Lovers,' no extraordinary play, methinks, and thence to Drumbleby's, and there did talk a great deal about pipes ; and did buy a recorder, which

I do intend to learn to play on, the sound of it being, of all sounds in the world, most pleasing to me." [Pepys, *8th April*, 1668.]

"Lieutenant Lambert and I to the Exchange, and thence to an ordinary over against it, where to our dinner we had a fellow play well upon the bagpipes, and whistle like a bird exceeding well, and I had a fancy to learn to whistle as he do, and did promise to come some other day, and give him an angell to teach me." [Pepys, *17th May*, 1661.]

Evelyn, also, was interested in instrumental music : "To our Society. There was brought a new-invented instrument of music, being a harpsichord with gut-strings, sounding like a concert of viols with an organ, made vocal by a wheel, and a zone of parchment that rubbed horizontally against the strings." [Evelyn, *5th October*, 1664.]

"I dined with Mr. Slingsby, Master of the Mint, with my wife, invited to hear music, which was exquisitely performed by four of the most renowned masters : Du Prue, a Frenchman, on the lute ; Signor Bartholomeo, an Italian, on the harpsichord ; Nicholao on the violin ; but, above all, for its sweetness and novelty, the *viol d'amore* of five wire strings played on with a bow, being but an ordinary violin, played on lyre-way, by a German. There was also a *flute douce*, now in much request for accompanying the voice. Mr. Slingsby, whose son and daughter played skilfully, had these meetings frequently in his house." [Evelyn, *20th November*, 1679.]

Of all its various phases it was the vocal form of music which charmed Pepys most. Their ability to sing influenced him even in the choice of his servants, and his family circle must at times have presented a happy and interesting spectacle as he delighted them with his " Beauty, Retire," and they joined him in part singing.

" Long with Mr. Berkenshaw in the morning at my musique practice, finishing my song of ' Gaze not on swans,' in two parts, which pleases me well, and I did give him £5 for this month or five weeks that he hath taught me, which is a great deal of money, and troubled me to part with it." [Pepys, *24th February*, 1662.]

" I spent the afternoon upon a song of Solyman's words to Roxalana that I have set, and so with my wife walked and Mercer to Mrs. Pierce's, where Captain Rolt and Mrs. Knipp, Mr. Coleman and his wife, and Laneare, Mrs. Worshipp and her singing daughter, met ; and by and by, unexpectedly comes Mr. Pierce from Oxford. Here the best company for musique I ever was in, in my life, and wish I could live and die in it, both for musique and the face of Mrs. Pierce, and my wife, and Knipp, who is pretty enough ; but the most excellent, mad-humoured thing, and sings the noblest that ever I heard in my life, and Rolt, with her, some things together, most excellently. I spent the night in an extasy almost ; and, having invited them to my house a day or two hence, we broke up." [Pepys, *6th December*, 1665.]

" To Mr. Hill, and sang, among other things, my song of ' Beauty, retire,' which he likes, only excepts against two notes in the base, but likes the whole very well." [Pepys, *9th December*, 1665.]

" Home, and there I find Gosnell come, who, my wife tells me, is like to prove a pretty companion, of which I am glad, and who sings exceeding well, and I shall take great delight in her." [Pepys, 5th December, 1662.]

" Spent all the afternoon, Pelling, Howe, and I, and my boy, singing of Lock's response to the Ten Commandments, which he hath set very finely, and was a good while since sung before the King, and spoiled in the performance, which occasoned his printing them for his vindication, and are excellent good." [Pepys, 1st September, 1667.]

" To Mr. Barlow at his lodgings at the Golden Eagle, in the new street between Fetter Lane and Shoe Lane. Dined at a club, where we had three voices to sing catches." [Pepys, 21st July, 1660.]

" The play being done, I took the women, and Mrs. Corbett, who was with them, by coach, it raining, to Mrs. Manuel's, the Jew's widow, formerly a player, who we heard sing with one of the Italians that was there ; and, indeed, she sings mightily well, and just after the Italian manner, but yet do not please me like one of Mrs. Knipp's songs, to a good English tune, the manner of their ayre not pleasing me so well as the fashion of our own, nor so natural." [Pepys, 12th August, 1667.]

" Sir W. Pen and I went out with Sir R. Slingsby to bowles in his ally, and there had good sport. I took my flageolette, and played upon the leads in the garden, where Sir W. Pen come out in his shirt into his leads, and there we staid talking and singing and drinking great draughts of claret, and eating botargo, and bread and butter till twelve at night, it being moonshine ; and so to bed, very near fuddled." [Pepys, 5th June, 1661.]

General Activities.

Pepys gives interesting sidelights on general domestic life. If one judges by the next two extracts the diarist was not over-scrupulous about personal cleanliness : " My wife busy in going with her woman to the hot-house to bathe herself, after her long being within doors in the dirt, so that she now pretends to a resolution of being hereafter very clean. How long it will hold I can guess." [Pepys, 21*st February*, 1665.]

" Late home, and to clean myself with warm water ; my wife will have me, because she do use it herself." [Pepys, 25*th December*, 1665.]

One hears of the wrongs of a husband being righted by his fellows : " Down to Greenwich, where I find the stairs full of people, there being a great riding there to-day for a man, the constable of the town, whose wife beat him." [Pepys, 10*th June*, 1667.]

A master was welcomed by making his servants drunk : " I went with Lord Howard of Norfolk to visit Sir William Ducie at Charlton, where we dined : the servants made our coachmen so drunk that they both fell off their boxes on the heath, where we were fain to leave them, and were driven to London by two servants of my Lord's. This barbarous custom of making the masters welcome by intoxicating the servants had now the second time happened to my coach-men." [Evelyn, 18*th March*, 1669.]

Charms as cures were held in high esteem :

" A THORNE.

" Jesus, that was of a Virgin born,
" Was pricked both with nail and thorn ;
" It neither wealed, nor belled, rankled nor boned ;
" In the name of Jesus no more shall this.

" Or, thus :—

" Christ was of a Virgin born,
" And he was pricked with a thorn ;
" And it did neither bell, nor swell ;
" And I trust in Jesus this never will.

" A CRAMP.
" Cramp be thou faintless,
" As our Lady was sinless,
" When she bare Jesus.

" A BURNING.
" There came three Angells out of the East ;
" The one brought fire, the other brought frost—
" Out fire ; in frost,
" In the name of the Father, and Son, and Holy
    Ghost. Amen." [Pepys, 31*st December*, 1664.]

" Homeward, in my way buying a hare, and
taking it home, which arose upon my discourse
to-day with Mr. Batten, in Westminster Hall,
who showed me my mistake that my hare's foot
hath not the joynt to it ; and assures me he never
had his cholique since he carried it about him :
and it is a strange thing how fancy works for I
no sooner handled his foot, but I become very well,
and so continue." [Pepys, 20*th January*, 1665.]

Christenings, weddings and funerals were social
events which Pepys did not miss : " To Lovett's
house, where I stood godfather. But it was pretty,
that, being a Protestant, a man stood by and was
my Proxy to answer for me. A priest christened
it, and the boy's name is Samuel. The ceremonies
many, and some foolish. The priest in a gentleman's
dress, more than my own ; but is a Capuchin,
one of the Queen-mother's priests. He did give

my proxy and the woman proxy, my Lady Bills, absent, had a proxy also, good advice to bring up the child ; and, at the end, that he ought never to marry the child nor the godmother, nor the god-mother the child or the godfather : but, which is strange, they say the mother of the child and the godfather may marry. By and by the Lady Bills come in, a well-bred but crooked woman. The poor people of the house had good wine, and a good cake ; and she a pretty woman in her lying-in dress. It cost me near 40s. the whole christening : to mid-wife 20s., nurse 10s., maid 2s. 6d., and the coach 5s." [Pepys, 18th October, 1666.]

" To church in the morning, and there saw a wedding in the church, which I have not seen many a day ; and the young people so merry one with another ! and strange to see what delight we married people have to see these poor fools decoyed into our condition, every man and woman gazing and smiling at them." [Pepys, 25th December, 1665.]

" To dinner to Sir W. Pen's, it being a solemn feast day with him—his wedding day, and we had, besides a good chine of beef and other good cheer, eighteen mince pies in a dish, the number of years that he hath been married." [Pepys, 6th January, 1662.]

" Up betimes, and walked to my brother's, where a great while putting things in order against anon ; and so to Wotton, my shoemaker, and there got a pair of shoes blacked on the soles against anon for me : so to my brother's. To church, and, with the grave-maker, chose a place for my brother to lie in, just under my mother's pew. But to see how a man's tombes are at the mercy of such a fellow, that for sixpence he would, as his own words were, ' I will justle them together but I will make room for him ; ' speaking of the fulness of the middle aisle, where he was to lie ; and that he would, for my father's sake, do my brother, that is dead, all the civility he can ; which was to disturb other corps that are not quite rotten, to make room for him ; and methought his manner of speaking it was very remarkable ; as of a thing that now was in his power to do a man a courtesy or not. I dressed myself, and so did my servant Besse ; and so to my brother's again : whither, though invited, as the custom is, at one or two o'clock, they come not till four or five. But, at last, one after another, they come, many more than I bid : and my reckoning that I bid was one hundred and twenty ; but I believe there was nearer one hundred and fifty. Their service was six biscuits a-piece, and what they pleased of burnt claret. My cozen Joyce Norton kept the wine and cakes above ; and did give out to them that served, who had white gloves given them. But, above all, I am beholden to Mrs. Holden, who was most kind, and did take mighty pains not only in getting the house and every thing else ready, but this day in going up and down to see the house filled and served, in order to mine and their great content, I think : the men sitting by themselves in some rooms, and the women by themselves in others, very close, but yet room enough. Anon to church, walking out into the street to the conduit, and so across the street ; and had a very good company along with the corps. And, being come to the grave as above, Dr. Pierson, the minister of the parish, did read the service for buriall : and so I saw my poor brother laid into the grave : and so all broke up ; and I and my wife, and Madam Turner and her family, to her brother's, and by and by fell to a barrell of oysters, cake, and cheese, of Mr. Honiwood's, with him, in his chamber and below, being too merry for so late a sad work. But, Lord ! to see how the world makes nothing of the memory of a man, an hour after he is dead ! And, indeed, I must blame myself ; for, though at the sight of him dead and dying, I had real grief for a while, while he was in my sight, yet presently after, and ever since, I have had very little grief indeed for him." [Pepys, 18*th March*, 1664.]

" To Mrs. Turner's, where I find her and her sister Dike very sad for the death of their brother. After a little common expression of sorrow, Mrs. Turner told me that the trouble she would put me to was, to consult about getting an achievement prepared, scutcheons were done already, to set over the door. Come Smith to me, with whom I did agree for £4 to make a handsome one, all square within the frame." [Pepys, 17*th December*, 1663.]

Outdoor Amusements.

Both diarists have countless records of outdoor amusements, of bowls and ninepins, of wrestling and morris-dancing, of football and pall-mall, etc. Many of these were healthy British games : " To the Tennis Court, and there saw the King play at tennis and others : but to see how the King's play was extolled, without any cause at all, was a loathsome sight, though sometimes, indeed, he did play very well, and deserved to be commended ;

but such open flattery is beastly. Afterwards
to St. James's Park, seeing people play at
Pell Mell ; where it pleased me mightily to hear a
gallant lately come from France, swear at one
of his companions for suffering his man, a spruce
blade, to be so saucy as to strike a ball while his
master was playing on the Mall.'' [Pepys, *4th
January*, 1664.]

" I walked in the Parke, discoursing with the
keeper of the Pell Mell, who was sweeping of it ;
who told me of what the earth is mixed that do
floor the Mall, and that over all there is cockle-
shells powdered, and spread to keep it fast ; which,
however, in dry weather, turns to dust and deads
the ball.'' [Pepys, *15th May*, 1663.]

" Having seen the strange and wonderful dexterity of the sliders on the new canal in St. James's
Park, performed before their Majesties by divers
gentlemen and others with skates, after the manner
of the Hollanders, with what swiftness they pass,
how suddenly they stop in full career upon the
ice ; I went home by water, but not without exceeding difficulty; the Thames being frozen, great
flakes of ice encompassing our boat.'' [Evelyn,
1st December, 1662.]

" I went with my wife to Conflans, where were
abundance of ladies and others bathing in the
river ; the ladies had their tents spread on the
water for privacy.'' [Evelyn, *2nd August*, 1651.]

" I sailed this morning with his Majesty in one
of his yachts (or pleasure-boats), vessels not known
among us till the Dutch East India Company
presented that curious piece to the King ; being
very excellent sailing vessels. It was on a wager
between his other new pleasure-boat, built frigate-

like, and one of the Duke of York's ; the wager
100l. ; the race from Greenwich to Gravesend and
back. The King lost it going, the wind being contrary, but saved stakes in returning. There were
divers noble persons and lords on board, his Majesty
sometime steering himself. His barge and kitchen
boat attended. I brake fast this morning with the
King at return in his smaller vessel, he being pleased
to take me and only four more, who were noblemen, with him ; but dined in his yacht, where we
all eat together with his Majesty." [Evelyn, *1st
October*, 1661.]

"But after dinner was all our sport, when there
come in a juggler, who, indeed, did shew us so good
tricks as I have never seen in my life, I think, of
legerdemaine, and such as my wife hath since
seriously said that she would not believe but that
he did them by the help of the devil." [Pepys,
24th May, 1667.]

Into other sports crept the money element :
" Abroad, and stopped at Bear-garden stairs,
there to see a prize fought. But the house so full
there was no getting in there, so forced to go through
an ale-house into the pit, where the bears are
baited ; and upon a stool did see them fight,
which they did very furiously, a butcher and a
waterman. The former had the better all along,
till by and by the latter dropped his sword out of
his hand, and the butcher, whether not seeing his
sword dropped I know not, but did give him a cut
over the wrist, so as he was disabled to fight any
longer. But, Lord ! to see how in a minute the
whole stage was full of watermen to revenge the
foul play, and the butchers to defend their fellow,
though most blamed him ; and there they all fell

to it to knocking down and cutting many on each
side. It was pleasant to see, but that I stood in
the pit, and feared that in the tumult I might get
some hurt. At last the battle broke up, and so
I away."] Pepys, 27th May 1667.]

"The towne talk this day is of nothing but the
great foot-race run this day on Banstead Downes,
between Lee, the Duke of Richmond's footman,
and a tyler, a famous runner. And Lee hath beat
him; though the King and Duke of York and all
men almost did bet three or four to one upon the
tyler's head." [Pepys, 30th July, 1663.]

Unfortunately many of the sports were brutal.
Evelyn is frankly disgusted at such barbarity as
cock-fighting, bull-baiting, etc. So is Pepys, but
he is present at the meetings!

"There was now a very gallant horse to be
baited to death with dogs; but he fought them
all, so as the fiercest of them could not fasten on
him, till the men run him through with their swords.
This wicked and barbarous sport deserved to have
been punished in the cruel contrivers to get money,
under pretence that the horse had killed a man,
which was false. I would not be persuaded to
be a spectator." [Evelyn, 17th August, 1667.]

"To Shoe Lane, to see a cocke-fighting at a
new pit there, a spot I was never at in my life:
but Lord! to see the strange variety of people,
from Parliament man, by name Wildes, that was
Deputy Governor of the Tower when Robinson
was Lord Mayor, to the poorest 'prentices, bakers,
brewers, butchers, draymen, and what not; and
all these fellows one with another cursing and
betting. I soon had enough of it. It is strange to
see how people of this poor rank, that look as if

they had not bread to put in their mouths, shall
bet three or four pounds at a time, and lose it, and
yet bet as much the next battle ; so that one of
them will lose 10 or £20 at a meeting." [Pepys,
21st December, 1663.]

"I to the new Cocke-pitt by the King's gate,
and there saw the manner of it, and the mixed
rabble of people that come thither, and saw two
battles of cocks, wherein is no great sport, but only
to consider how these creatures, without any
provocation, do fight and kill one another, and
aim only at one another's heads." [Pepys, 6th
April, 1668.]

"I went with some friends to the Bear Garden
where was cock-fighting, dog-fighting, bear and
bull-baiting, it being a famous day for all these
butcherly sports, or rather barbarous cruelties.
The bulls did exceeding well, but the Irish wolf-
dog exceeded, which was a tall greyhound, a stately
creature indeed, who beat a cruel mastiff. One
of the bulls tossed a dog full into a lady's lap as
she sate in one of the boxes at a considerable
height from the arena. Two poor dogs were killed,
and so all ended with the ape on horseback, and
I most heartily weary of the rude and dirty pastime,
which I had not seen, I think, in twenty years
before." [Evelyn, 16th June, 1670.]

Pepys has a similar experience which he describes
as " good sport " and yet " nasty pleasure." He
ends the evening in pleasanter occupations : " After
dinner, with my wife and Mercer to the Beare
Garden ; where I have not been, I think, of many
years, and saw some good sport of the bull's
tossing the dogs—one into the very boxes. But
it is a very rude and nasty pleasure. We had a

great many hectors in the same box with us, and one very fine went into the pit, and played his dog for a wager ; which was a strange sport for a gentleman ; where they drank wine, and drank Mercer's health first ; which I pledged with my hat off. We supped at home, and very merry. And then about nine to Mrs. Mercer's gate, where the fire and boys expected us, and her son had provided abundance of serpents and rockets ; and there mighty merry, my Lady Pen and Pegg going thither with us, and Nan Wright, till about twelve at night, flinging our fireworks, and burning one another, and the people over the way. And, at last, our business being most spent, we went into Mrs. Mercer's, and there mighty merry, smutting one another with candle grease and soot, till most of us were like devils. And that being done, then we broke up, and to my house ; and there I made them drink, and upstairs we went, and then fell into dancing, W. Batelier dancing well ; and dressing, him and I, and one Mr. Banister, who, with my wife, come over also with us, like women ; and Mercer put on a suit of Tom's, like a boy, and mighty mirth we had, and Mercer danced a jigg ; and Nan Wright and my wife and Pegg Pen put on perriwigs. Thus we spent till three or four in the morning, mighty merry ; and then parted, and to bed." [Pepys, *14th August*, 1666.]

Shows and fairs were much in evidence :

" Going to London, my Lord Mayor's show stopped me in Cheapside ; one of the pageants represented a great wood, with the royal oak, and history of his Majesty's miraculous escape at Boscobel." [Evelyn, *29th October*, 1660.]

" But, Lord ! to see how my nature could not

refrain from the temptation ; but I must invite them to go to Foxhall, to Spring Gardens, though I had freshly received minutes of a great deal of extraordinary business. However, I sent them before with Creed, and I did some of my business ; and so after them, and find them there, in an arbour, and had met with Mrs. Pierce, and some company with her. So here I spent 20s. upon them, and were pretty merry. Among other things, had a fellow that imitated all manner of birds, and dogs, and hogs, with his voice, which was mighty pleasant. Staid here till night : then set Mrs. Pierce in at the New Exchange ; and ourselves took coach, and so set Mrs. Horsly home, and then home ourselves, but with great trouble in the streets, by bonfires, it being the King's birth-day and day of Restoration." [Pepys, 29th May, 1666.]

" To Southwarke-Fair, very dirty, and there saw the puppet-show of Whittington, which was pretty to see ; and how that idle thing do work upon people that see it, and even myself too ! And thence to Jacob Hall's dancing on the ropes, where I saw such action as I never saw before, and mightily worth seeing ; and here took acquaintance with a fellow that carried me to a tavern, whither come the musick of this booth, and by and by Jacob Hall himself, with whom I had a mind to speak, to hear whether he had ever any mischief by falls in his time. He told me, ' Yes, many, but never to the breaking of a limb : ' he seems a mighty strong man." [Pepys, 21st September, 1668.]

A most curious show was seen on the frozen Thames in the early days of 1684 : " The frost continuing more and more severe, the Thames before London was still planted with booths in formal streets, all sorts of trades and shops furnished, and full of commodities, even to a printing-press, where the people and ladies took a fancy to have their names printed, and the day and year set down when printed on the Thames : this humour took so universally, that it was estimated the printer gained £5 a day, for printing a line only, at sixpence a name, besides what he got by ballads, &c. Coaches plied from Westminster to the Temple, and from several other stairs to and fro, as in the streets, sleds, sliding with skates, a bull-baiting, horse and coach-races, puppet-plays and interludes, cooks, tippling, and other lewd places, so that it seemed to be a bacchanalian triumph, or carnival on the water, whilst it was a severe judgment on the land, the trees not only splitting as if lightning-struck, but men and cattle perishing in divers places, and the very seas so locked up with ice, that no vessels could stir out or come in. The fowls, fish, and birds, and all our exotic plants and greens, universally perishing. Many parks of deer were destroyed, and all sorts of fuel so dear, that there were great contributions to preserve the poor alive. Nor was this severe weather much less intense in most parts of Europe, even as far as Spain and the most southern tracts. London, by reason of the excessive coldness of the air hindering the ascent of the smoke, was so filled with the fuliginous steam of the sea-coal, that hardly could one see across the streets, and this filling the lungs with its gross particles, exceedingly obstructed the breast, so as one could scarcely breathe. Here was no water to be had from the pipes and engines, nor could the brewers and divers other trades-men work, and every moment was full of disastrous accidents." [Evelyn, *24th January*, 1684.]

The Theatre.

One amusement, theatre-going, merits special mention, for Pepys has much to say with regard to it. If frequent attendance at the theatre be taken as a criterion, Pepys was eminently fitted to enlighten us, for he records well over three hundred performances which he witnessed, giving an average of one visit every eleven days. Evelyn was disgusted at the wickedness of the stage and was seldom seen there.

" To a new play with several of my relations, *The Evening Lover*, a foolish plot, and very profane ; it afflicted me to see how the stage was degenerated and polluted by the licentious times." [Evelyn, *19th June*, 1668.]

The Puritans had succeeded in closing the theatres from 1642 to 1660 but with the restoration of Charles II. they were re-opened, and patronised by King and people alike. The first problem confronting the theatre managers was the provision of plays. For a start there were Shakespeare's plays, though occasionally these were " amended " for stage purposes. Pepys saw a good dozen different Shakespearean plays and his remarks on some are interesting : " This day my oaths for drinking of wine and going to plays are out ; and so I do resolve to take a liberty to-day, and then to fall to them again. To Mr. Coventry's, and so with him and Sir W. Pen up to the Duke, where the King come also, and staid till the Duke was ready. It being Collar-day, we had no time to talk with him about any business. To the King's Theatre, where we

saw *Midsummer's Night's Dream*, which I had never
seen before, nor shall ever again, for it is the most
insipid, ridiculous play that ever I saw in my
life." [Pepys, *29th September*, 1662.]

"My wife and I by coach, first to see my little
picture that is a-drawing, and thence to the Opera,
and then saw *Romeo and Juliet*, the first time it
was ever acted, but it is a play of itself the worst
that ever I heard, and the worst acted that ever
I saw these people do, and I am resolved to go no
more to see the first time of acting, for they were all
of them out more or less." [Pepys, *1st March*, 1662.]

"To the Duke's house, and there saw *Twelfth-
Night* acted well, though it be but a silly play, and
not relating at all to the name or day." [Pepys,
6th February, 1663.]

"Went to the Duke's house, the first play I
have been at these six months, according to my last
vowe, and here saw the so much cried-up play of
Henry the Eighth, which, though I went with
resolution to like it, is so simple a thing, made up
of a great many patches, that, besides the shows
and processions in it, there is nothing in the world
good or well done." [Pepys, *1st January*, 1664.]

"Mr. Creed dining with me, I got him to give
my wife and me a play this afternoon, lending him
money to do it, which is a fallacy that I have found
now once, to avoid my vowe with, but never to
be more practised, I swear. To the new play, at the
Duke's house, of *Henry the Fifth*; a most noble
play, writ by my Lord Orrery; wherein Betterton,
Harris, and Ianthe's parts are most incomparably
wrote and done, and the whole play the most full
of height and raptures of wit and sense that ever
I heard; having but one incongruity, that King

Harry promises to plead for Tudor to their mistress, Princess Katherine of France, more than, when it comes to it, he seems to do ; and Tudor refused by her with some kind of indignity, not with a difficulty and honour that it ought to have been done in to him." [Pepys, 13th August, 1664.]

"To the Duke's house, and saw *Macbeth*, which, though I saw it lately, yet appears a most excellent play in all respects, but especially in divertisement, though it be a deep tragedy ; which is a strange perfection in a tragedy, it being most proper here, and suitable." [Pepys, 8th January, 1666.]

"To the Duke of York's house, and there saw the *Tempest* again, which is very pleasant, and full of so good variety, that I cannot be more pleased almost in a comedy, only the seaman's part a little too tedious." [Pepys, 13th November, 1667.]

The works of other Elizabethan or pre-Restoration dramatists such as Marlowe, Massinger, Dekker, Middleton, Heywood, Shirley, Ford, Jonson, Beaumont and Fletcher, were now seen on the stage : "Then to the Theatre, *The Alchymist*, which is a most incomparable play." [Pepys, 22nd June, 1661.]

"At noon, he, with Sir W. Pen and his daughter, dined with me, and he to his work again, and we by coach to the Theatre, and saw *Love in a Maze*. The play hath little in it, but Lacy's part of a country-fellow, which he did to admiration." [Pepys, 22nd May, 1662.]

"To the Duke's play-house, where we saw *The Duchess of Malfy* well performed, but Betterton and Ianthe [Mrs. Betterton] to admiration. Strange to see how easily my mind do revert to its former practice of loving plays and wine ; but this night

I have again bound myself to Christmas next."
[*Pepys, 30th September, 1662.*]

Plays were also imported, especially from
France.

" This done, we broke up, and I to the Cockpitt,
with much crowding and waiting, where I saw
The Valiant Cidd acted—a play I have read with
great delight, but is a most dull thing acted, which
I never understood before, there being no pleasure
in it, though done by Betterton and by Ianthe,
and another fine wench that is come in the room of
Roxalana ; nor did the King or Queene once
smile all the whole play, nor any of the whole
company seem to take any pleasure, but what was
in the greatness and gallantry of the company."
[*Pepys, 1st December, 1662.*]

But a new type of play was developing : " I saw
Hamlet, Prince of Denmark played ; but now the
old plays began to disgust this refined age, since
his Majesty's being so long abroad." [*Evelyn,
26th November, 1661.*]

In tragedy it was the last two sources, French and
Elizabethan, which were producing a bombastic
kind of verse drama called the heroic tragedy.
Similar influences were at work producing the
witty but scandalous Restoration comedy. The
new movement can be exemplified by Dryden : " To
the King's Theatre, and there saw the *Indian
Queene* acted ; which indeed is a most pleasant
show, and beyond my expectation ; the play good,
but spoiled with the ryme, which breaks the
sense. But above my expectation most, the eldest
Marshall did do her part most excellently well as
I ever heard woman in my life ; but her voice
is not so sweet as Ianthe's ; but, however, we come

home mightily contented." [Pepys, *1st February*, 1664.]

"With my Lord Brouncker and his mistress to the King's playhouse, and there saw *The Indian Emperour*: where I find Nell come again, which I am glad of; but was most infinitely displeased with her being put to act the Emperour's daughter, which is a great and serious part, which she does most basely. The rest of the play, though pretty good, was not well acted by most of them, methought; so that I took no great content in it." [Pepys, *22nd August*, 1667.]

"The play being done, we took coach, and to Court, and there saw *The Wilde Gallant* performed by the King's house, but it was ill acted, and the play so poor a thing as I never saw in my life almost, and so little answering the name, that, from the beginning to the end, I could not, nor can, at this time, tell certainly which was the Wild Gallant. The King did not seem pleased at all, the whole play, nor any body else. My lady Castlemaine was all worth seeing to-night, and little Steward." [Pepys, *23rd January*, 1663.]

Ladies had often to hide their feelings behind masks: "To the Royal Theatre; and there saw *The Committee*, a merry but indifferent play, only Lacy's part, an Irish footman, is beyond imagination. Here I saw my Lord Falconbridge, and his lady, my Lady Mary Cromwell, who looks as well as I have known her, and well clad: but when the house began to fill, she put on her vizard, and so kept it on all the play; which of late is become a great fashion among the ladies, which hides their whole face. So to the Exchange, to buy things

with my wife ; among others, a vizard for herself."
[Pepys, 12th June, 1663.]

It was at this time that opera made its appearance in England : " Went to Sir William Davenant's Opera ; this being the fourth day that it hath begun, and the first that I have seen it. To-day was acted the second part of *The Siege of Rhodes*. We staid a very great while for the King and Queen of Bohemia ; and by the breaking of a board over our heads, we had a great deal of dust fell into the ladies' necks and the men's haire, which made good sport. The King being come, the scene opened ; which indeed is very fine and magnificent, and well acted, all but the Eunuche, who was so much out that he was hissed off the stage." [Pepys, 2nd July, 1661.]

At the Restoration, two troops of actors were formed by royal authority, one called the Duke's, under the direction of Sir William Davenant, and the other the King's, whose patentee was Thomas Killigrew. Pepys favoured the Duke's players, perhaps because his favourite actor, Betterton, was a member of this company : " To the Opera, and there saw *Hamlet, Prince of Denmarke*, done with scenes very well, but above all, Betterton did the Prince's part beyond imagination." [Pepys, 24th August, 1661.]

" Here I met Rolt and Sir John Chichly, and I met Harris, the player, and talked of *Catiline*, which is to be suddenly acted at the King's house ; and there all agree that it cannot be well done at that house, there not being good actors enough : and Burt acts Cicero, which they all conclude he will not be able to do well. The King gives them £500 for robes, there being, as they say, to be sixteen scarlet robes." [Pepys, 11th December, 1667.]

But Pepys was perhaps even more interested in the actresses, who were now seen on the stage for the first time. Betterton's wife, who performed *Ianthe* in Davenant's *Siege of Rhodes*, Elizabeth Davenport, who took *Roxalana* in the same play, Nell Gwynn, the Marshalls, and a Mrs. Knipp, who was a member of the King's Company, had their share of praise from the diarist : the last named was on intimate terms with him : " To the King's house : and there, going in, met with Knipp, and she took us up into the tireing-rooms : and to the women's shift, where Nell was dressing herself, and was all unready, and is very pretty, prettier than I thought. And into the scene-room, and there sat down, and she gave us fruit : and here I read the questions to Knipp, while she answered me, through all her part of *Flora Figarys*, which was acted to-day. But, Lord ! to see how they were both painted would make a man mad, and did make me loath them ; and what base company of men comes among them, and how lewdly they talk ! and how poor the men are in clothes, and yet what a show they make on the stage by candle-light, is very observable. But to see how Nell cursed, for having so few people in the pit, was pretty ; the other house carrying away all the people at the new play, and is said, now-a-days, to have generally most company, as being better players. By and by into the pit, and there saw the play, which is pretty good." [Pepys, 5th October, 1667.]

"After dinner, with my wife, to the King's house to see *The Maiden Queene*, a new play of

Dryden's, mightily commended for the regularity
of it, and the strain and wit ; and, the truth is,
there is a comical part done by Nell, which is
Florimell, that I never can hope ever to see the
like done again, by man or woman. The King and
Duke of York were at the play. But so great
performance of a comical part was never, I believe,
in the world before as Nell do this, both as a mad
girle, then most and best of all when she comes in
like a young gallant ; and hath the motions and
carriage of a spark the most that ever I saw any
man have. It makes me, I confess, admire her."
[Pepys, *2nd March*, 1667.]

"To the King's house, where going in for Knipp,
the play being done, I did see Beck Marshall come
dressed, off of the stage, and look mighty fine, and
pretty, and noble : and also Nell, in her boy's
clothes, mighty pretty. But, Lord ! their confi-
dence ! and how many men do hover about them
as soon as they come off the stage, and how confident they are in their talk ! " [Pepys, *7th May*,
1668.]

"Knipp's maid comes to me, to tell me that the
women's day at the playhouse is to-day, and that
therefore I must be there, to encrease their profit.
I did give the pretty maid Betty that comes to me,
half-a-crown for coming, and had a kiss or two—
elle being mighty *jolie*." [Pepys, *28th August*, 1668.]

Another set of actors, not so experienced as the
two regular companies, commenced producing
plays in Lincoln's Inn Fields. Their theatre was
known as the Nursery : " To the Nursery, where
none of us ever were before ; the house is better and
the musick better than we looked for, and the
acting not much worse, because I expected as

bad as could be : and I was not much mistaken, for it was so. Their play was a bad one, called *Jeronimo is Mad Again*, a tragedy. Here was some good company by us, who did make mighty sport at the folly of their acting, which I could not refrain from sometimes, though I was sorry for it. I was prettily served this day at the play-house door, where, giving six shillings into the fellow's hand for three of us, the fellow by legerdemain did convey one away, and with so much grace faced me down that I did give him but five, that, though I knew the contrary, yet I was over-powered by his so grave and serious demanding the other shilling, that I could not deny him, but was forced by myself to give it him." [Pepys, 24*th February*, 1668.]

The Elizabethan theatre was simply an enclosed yard ; in Pepys's time some theatres were roofed though not always very adequately : " To the King's playhouse, and there saw *The Surprizall* ; and a disorder in the pit by its raining in, from the cupola at top." [Pepys, 1*st May*, 1668.]

Performances at the public theatres generally took place in the afternoon ; those at Court were held at night : " To Hercules-Pillars, and there dined, and thence to the Duke of York's playhouse, at a little past twelve, to get a good place in the pit, against the new play, and there setting a poor man to keep my place, I out, and spent an hour at Martin's, my booksellers, and so back again, where I find the House quite full." [Pepys, 2*nd May*, 1668.]

" In the evening to White Hall, and there did without much trouble get into the playhouse, finding a good place among the Ladies of Honour, and all of us sitting in the pit ; and then by and by came the King and Queen, and they began *Bartholomew Fair*. But I like no play here so well as at the common playhouse." [Pepys, *22nd February*, 1669.]

Prices of admittance were high : " Thence I after dinner to the Duke of York's playhouse, and there saw *Sir Martin Mar-all ;* which I have seen so often, and yet am mightily pleased with it, and think it mighty witty, and the fullest of proper matter for mirth that ever was writ ; and I do clearly see that they do improve in their acting of it. Here a mighty company of citizens, 'prentices, and others ; and it makes me observe, that when I began first to be able to bestow a play on myself, I do not remember that I saw so many by half of the ordinary 'prentices and mean people in the pit at 2s. 6d. a-piece as now ; I going for several years no higher than the 12d. and then the 18d. places, though I strained hard to go in when I did : so much the vanity and prodigality of the age is to be observed in this particular." [Pepys, *1st January*, 1668.]

" Full of my desire of seeing my Lord Orrery's new play this afternoon at the King's house, *The Black Prince*, the first time it is acted ; where, though we came by two o'clock, yet there was no room in the pit, but were forced to go into one of the upper boxes, at 4s. a piece, which is the first time I ever sat in a box in my life." [Pepys, *19th October*, 1667.]

Glimpses of the interior are given : " After dinner, we walked to the King's playhouse, all in dirt, they being altering of the stage to make it wider. But God knows when they will begin to act again ; but my business here was to see the inside of the stage and all the tiring-rooms and machines ; and, indeed, it was a sight worthy seeing. But to see their clothes, and the various sorts, and what a mixture of things there was ; here a wooden leg, there a ruff, here a hobby-horse, there a crown, would make a man split himself to see with laughing ; and particularly Lacy's wardrobe, and Shotrell's. But then again to think how fine they show on the stage by candle-light, and how poor things they are to look at too near hand, is not pleasant at all. The machines are fine, and the paintings very pretty." [Pepys, 19th March, 1666.]

" This done, T. Killigrew and I to talk : and he tells me how the audience at his house is not above half so much as it used to be before the late fire. That Knipp is like to make the best actor that ever come upon the stage, she understanding so well : that they are going to give her £30 a year more. That the stage is now by his pains a thousand times better and more glorious than ever heretofore. Now, wax-candles, and many of them ; then, not above 3lbs. of tallow : now, all things civil, no rudeness anywhere ; then, as in a bear-garden : then, two or three fiddlers ; now, nine or ten of the best : then, nothing but rushes upon the ground, and every thing else mean ; now, all otherwise : then, the Queen seldom and the King never would come ; now, not the King only for state, but all civil people do think they may come as well as any." [Pepys, 12th February, 1667.]

Oranges were a popular refreshment, one of the sellers, Orange Moll, being quite a noted character. Her wares were not always put to a legitimate use ! " Took coach, and called Mercer, and she and I to the Duke of York's playhouse, and there saw *The Tempest*, and between two acts, I went out to Mr. Harris, and got him to repeat to me the words of the Echo, while I writ them down, having tried in the play to have wrote them ; but, having done it without looking upon my paper, I find I could not read the blacklead. But now I have got the words clear, and, in going in thither, had the pleasure to see their actors in their several dresses, especially the seamen and monster, which were very droll : so into the play again. But there happened one thing which vexed me, which is, that the orange-woman did come in the pit, and challenge me for twelve oranges, which she de-livered by my order at a late play, at night, in order to give to some ladies in a box, which was wholly untrue, but yet she swore it to be true. But, however, I did deny it, and did not pay her ; but, for quiet, did buy 4s. worth of oranges of her, at 6d. a-piece." [Pepys, 11th May, 1668.]

" To the King's playhouse, and there saw *Henry the Fourth :* and contrary to expectation, was pleased in nothing more than in Cartwright's speaking of Falstaffe's speech about ' What is Honour ? ' The house full of Parliament-men, it being holyday with them : and it was observable how a gentleman of good habit, sitting just before us, eating of some fruit in the midst of the play, did drop down as dead, being choked ; but with much ado Orange Moll did thrust her finger down his throat, and brought him to life again." [Pepys, 2nd November, 1667.]

" It is about my Lady Harvy's being offended at Doll Common's acting of Sempronia, to imitate her ; for which she got my Lord Chamberlain, her kinsman, to imprison Doll : upon which my Lady Castlemaine made the King to release her, and to order her to act it again, worse than ever, the other day, where the King himself was ; and since it was acted again, and my Lady Harvy provided people to hiss her and fling oranges at her." [Pepys, 15*th January*, 1669.]

Travelling.

Travelling in the days of Pepys and Evelyn was difficult and any journey of more than a few miles was a test of endurance and courage.

Even in London the roads were bad : " I sat with the Commissioners about reforming buildings and streets of London, and we ordered the paving of the way from St. James's North, which was a quagmire, and also of the Haymarket about Piqudillo [Piccadilly], and agreed upon instructions to be printed and published for the better keeping the streets clean." [Evelyn, 31*st July*, 1662.]

Dangers were present as well as discomfort : " My wife come home, and seeming to cry ; for, bringing home in a coach her new ferrandin waistecoate, in Cheapside, a man asked her whether that was the way to the Tower ; and, while she was answering him, another, on the other side, snatched away her bundle out of her lap, and could not be recovered, but ran away with it, which vexes me cruelly, but it cannot be helped." [Pepys, 23*rd January*, 1663.]

" Being come hither, there waited for them their coach ; but, it being so late, I doubted what to do how to get them home. After half an hour's stay in the street, I sent my wife home by coach with

Mr. Creed's boy: and myself and Creed in the coach home with them. But, Lord! the fear that my Lady Paulina was in every step of the way: and indeed, at this time of the night, it was no safe thing to go that road; so that I was even afraid myself, though I appeared otherwise." [Pepys, 15*th June*, 1664.]

"By water to Woolwich, and walked back from Woolwich to Greenwich all alone; saw a man that had a cudgell in his hand, and, though he told me he laboured in the King's yard, and many other good arguments that he is an honest man, yet, God forgive me! I did doubt he might knock me on the head behind with his club." [Pepys, 30*th June*, 1664.]

At night the river was safer than the streets, for the only illumination until the end of the reign of Charles II. was by links or torches carried by "boys."

"So giving them a bottle or two of wine, I away with Payne, the waterman. He, seeking me at the play, did get a link to light me, and so light me to the Beare, where Bland, my waterman, waited for me with gold and other things he kept for me, to the value of £40 and more, which I had about me, for fear of my pockets being cut. So by link light through the bridge, it being mighty dark, but still weather, and so home." [Pepys, 21*st September*, 1668.]

Coaches, both public and private, were a great boon. Much to his delight, Pepys was able to procure a coach of his own: "Up betimes. Called by my tailor, and there first put on a summer suit this year; but it was not my fine one of flowered tabby vest, and coloured camelott tunique, because it was too fine with the gold lace at the bands, that I was afraid to be seen in it ; but put on the stuff suit I made the last year, which is now repaired ; and so did go to the Office in it, and sat all the morning, the day looking as if it would be fowle. At noon home to dinner, and there find my wife extraordinary fine, with her flowered tabby gown that she made two years ago, now laced exceeding pretty ; and, indeed, was fine all over ; and mighty earnest to go, though the day was very lowering ; and she would have me put on my fine suit, which I did. And so anon we went alone through the town with our new liveries of serge, and the horses' manes and tails tied with red ribbons, and the standards gilt with varnish, and all clean, and green reines, that people did mightily look upon us ; and, the truth is, I did not see any coach more pretty, though more gay, than our's, all the day. But we set out, out of humour—I because Betty, whom I expected, was not come to go with us ; and my wife that I would sit on the same seat with her, which she likes not, being so fine : and she then expected to meet Sheres, which we did in the Pell Mell, and, against my will, I was forced to take him into the coach, but was sullen all day almost, and little complaisant : the day being unpleasing, though the Park full of coaches, but dusty, and windy, and cold, and now and then a little dribbling of rain ; and, what made it worse, there were so many hackney-coaches as spoiled the sight of the gentlemen's ; and so we had little pleasure. But here was W. Batelier and his sister in a borrowed coach by themselves, and I took them and we to the lodge ; and at the door did give them a syllabub, and other things, cost me

12*s*., and pretty merry." [Pepys, 1*st May*, 1669.]

It was probably the uneven roads which led Pepys into the following amusing situation: " Thence home, and just at Holborne-Conduit the bolt broke, that holds the fore-wheels to the perch, and so the horses went away with them, and left the coachman and us ; but, being near our coach-maker's, and we staying in a little ironmonger's shop, we were presently supplied with another." [Pepys, 6*th February*, 1669.]

" A journey into the country was attended by even greater perils and discomforts. The roads were generally mere tracks, often without limits as regards width. Pepys made a tour through the West of England, meeting the usual experiences of lost ways and uncomfortable beds: " So out, and lost our way, but come into it again ; and in the evening betimes come to Reading." [Pepys, 16*th June*, 1668.]

" Up, finding our beds good, but lousy ; which made us merry." [Pepys, 12*th June*, 1668.]

This tour included a visit to Bath : " Having dined very well, 10*s*., we come before night to the Bath ; where I presently stepped out with my landlord, and saw the baths with people in them. They are not so large as I expected, but yet pleasant; and the town most of stone, and clean, though the streets generally narrow. I home, and being weary, went to bed without supper ; the rest supping.

" 13*th. Saturday*. Up at four o'clock, being by appointment called up to the Cross Bath ; where we were carried after one another, myself and wife and Betty Turner, Willet, and W. Hewer. And by and by, though we designed to have done before company come, much company come : very fine ladies ; and the manner pretty enough, only methinks it cannot be clean to go so many bodies together in the same water. Good conversation among them that are acquainted here, and stay together. Strange to see how hot the water is ; and in some places, though this is the most temperate bath, the springs so hot as the feet not able to endure. But strange to see when women and men here, that live all the season in these waters, cannot but be parboiled and look like the creatures of the bath ! Carried away wrapped in a sheet, and in a chair home ; and there one after another thus carried (I staying above two hours in the water) home to bed, sweating for an hour. And by and by comes musick to play to me, extraordinary good as ever I heard at London almost any where : 5s." [Pepys, 12th June, 1668, and 13th June, 1668.]

Evelyn, who was much more the traveller than Pepys, had several alarming experiences : " The weather being hot, and having sent my man on before, I rode negligently under favour of the shade, till, within three miles of Bromley, at a place called the Procession Oak, two cut-throats started out, and striking with long staves at the horse, and taking hold of the reins, threw me down, took my sword, and hauled me into a deep thicket, some quarter of a mile from the highway, where they might securely rob me, as they soon did. What they got of money, was not considerable, but they took two rings, the one an emerald with diamonds, the other an onyx, and a pair of buckles set with rubies and diamonds, which were of value, and after all bound my hands behind me, and my feet, having before pulled off my boots ; they then set me up against an oak, with most bloody threats to cut my throat if I offered to cry out, or make any noise ; for they should be within hearing, I not being the person they looked for. I told them that if they had not basely surprised me they should not have had so easy a prize, and that it would teach me never to ride near a hedge, since, had I been in the mid-way, they durst not have adventured on me ; at which they cocked their pistols, and told me they had long guns, too, and were fourteen companions. I begged for my onyx, told them it being engraved with my arms would betray them ; but nothing prevailed. My horse's bridle they slipped, and searched the saddle, which they pulled off, but let the horse graze, and then turning again bridled him and tied him to a tree, yet so as he might graze, and thus left me bound. My horse was perhaps not taken, because he was marked and cropped on both ears, and well known on that road. Left in this manner, grievously was I tormented with flies, ants, and the sun, nor was my anxiety little how I should get loose in that solitary place, where I could neither hear nor see any creature but my poor horse and a few sheep straggling in the copse.

"After near two hours attempting, I got my hands to turn palm to palm, having been tied back to back, and then it was long before I could slip the cord over my wrists to my thumb, which at last I did, and then soon unbound my feet, and saddling my horse and roaming a while about, I at last perceived dust to rise, and soon after heard the rattling of a cart, towards which I made, and, by the help of two countrymen, I got back into the highway. I rode to Colonel Blount's, a great justiciary of the times, who sent out hue and cry immediately. The next morning, sore as my wrists and arms were, I went to London, and got 500 tickets printed and dispersed by an officer of Goldsmiths' Hall, and within 2 days had tidings of all I had lost except my sword which had a silver hilt, and some trifles. The rogues had pawned one of my rings for a trifle to a goldsmith's servant before the tickets had came to the shop, by which meanes they scaped ; the other ring was bought by a victualler, who brought it to a goldsmith, but he having seen the ticket seized the man. I afterwards discharged him on his protestation of innocence. Thus did God deliver me from these villains, and not only so, but restored what they took, as twice before he had graciously done, both at sea and land ; I mean when I had been robbed by pirates, and was in danger of a considerable loss at Amsterdam ; for which, and many, many signal preservations, I am extremely obliged to give thanks to God my Saviour." [Evelyn, 11th June, 1652.]

Evelyn travelled extensively over Europe and discovered that travel abroad was even more dangerous than that at home, for there were pirates at sea as well as thieves on land: "At six in the evening, set sail for Calais ; the wind not favourable, I was very sea-sick, coming to an anchor about one o'clock ; about five in the morning, we had a long boat to carry us to land, though at a good distance ; this we willingly entered, because two vessels were chasing us ; but, being now almost at the harbour's mouth, through inadvertency there brake in upon us two such heavy seas, as had almost sunk the boat, I being near the middle up in water. Our steersman, it seems, apprehensive of the danger, was preparing to leap into the sea and trust to swimming, but seeing the vessel emerge, he put her into the pier, and so, God be thanked ! we got to Calais, though wet.

" Here I waited for company, the passage towards Paris being still infested with volunteers from the Spanish frontiers." [Evelyn, *13th August*, 1650.]

He was able to say on 8th February, 1661 : " This I made the *non ultra* of my travels, sufficiently sated with rolling up and down, and resolving within myself to be no longer an *individuum vagum*, if ever I got home again ; since, from the report of divers experienced and curious persons, I had been assured there was little more to be seen in the rest of the civil world, after Italy, France, Flanders, and the Low Countries, but plain and prodigious barbarism."

CHAPTER V

THE NATION AT WORSHIP

OUR last story, that of the nation at worship, shows a marked progress from the times when it was thought impossible to have political unity without religious unity, to those when toleration was an accepted practice.

Both diarists were zealous adherents of the Established Church though their attitudes towards church attendance varied greatly. Evelyn was devout ; it was to him a great privilege to partake of the Sacrament : " My birth-day, 54th year of of my life. Blessed be God ! It was also preparation-day for the Holy Sacrament, in which I participated the next day, imploring God's protection for the year following, and confirming my resolutions of a more holy life, even upon the Holy Book. The Lord assist and be gracious unto me ! Amen." [Evelyn, 31st October, 1674.]

Pepys was more secular in his outlook. Though his emotional nature was touched at times by the beauties of religion, his general behaviour at Church left much to be desired. He had little respect for the clergy : " Come Mr. Mills, the minister, to see me, which he hath rarely done to me, though every day almost to others of us, but he is a cunning fellow, and knows where the good victuals is, and the good drink, at Sir W. Batten's. However, I used him civilly, though I love him as I do the rest of his coat." [Pepys, 9th July, 1662.]

Church services gave opportunities to indulge in the vanities that are so characteristic of him:

"With my wife to church, and coming out, went out both before my Lady Batten, he not being there, which I believe will vex her." [Pepys, 28*th December*, 1662.]

They appealed to his insatiable curiosity.

"This morning, till churches were done, I spent going from one church to another, and hearing a bit here and a bit there." [Pepys, 16*th February*, 1662.]

They gave him opportunities even of love making! "I walked towards White Hall, but, being wearied, turned into St. Dunstan's Church, where I heard an able sermon of the minister of the place; and stood by a pretty, modest maid, whom I did labour to take by the hand; but she would not, but got further and further from me; and, at last, I could perceive her to take pins out of her pocket to prick me if I should touch her again—which, seeing, I did forbear, and was glad I did spy her design. And then I fell to gaze upon another pretty maid, in a pew close to me, and she on me; and I did go about to take her by the hand, which she suffered a little, and then withdrew. So the sermon ended, and the church broke up, and my amours ended also." [Pepys, 18*th August*, 1667.]

"After dinner I by water alone to Westminster to the parish Church, and did there entertain myself with my perspective glass up and down the church, by which I had the great pleasure of seeing and gazing at a great many very fine women; and what with that, and sleeping, I passed away the time till sermon was done." [Pepys, 26*th May*, 1667.]

Service was held in the morning and in the afternoon, the latter being an unfortunate time for the diarist after his heavy lunches : " At dinner, I took place of all but the Captain. After that, sermon again, at which I slept, God forgive me ! " [Pepys, 25*th March*, 1660.]

" After dinner to church again, my wife and I, where we had a dull sermon of a stranger, which made me sleep." [Pepys, 25*th December*, 1660.]

In 1662 the Church of England was restored to its position of supremacy, and Dissenters (Presbyterians as well as Roman Catholics) were persecuted. By the Act of Uniformity, all ministers by August 24*th*, 1662, must use the New Common Prayer Book of the Church of England or lose their posts : " This being the last Sunday that the Presbyterians are to preach, unless they read the new Common Prayer, and renounce the Covenant, I had a mind to hear Dr. Bates's farewell sermon ; and walked to St. Dunstan's, where, it not being seven o'clock yet, the doors were not open ; and so I walked an hour in the Temple-garden, reading my vows, which it is a great content to me to see how I am a changed man in all respects for the better, since I took them, which the God of Heaven continue to me, and make me thankful for. At eight o'clock I went, and crowded in at a back door among others, the church being half-full almost before any doors were open publicly, which is the first time that I have done so these many years ; and so got into the gallery, beside the pulpit, and heard very well. His text was, ' Now the God of Peace—— ; ' the last Hebrews, and the 20th verse : he making a very good sermon, and very little reflections in it to any thing of the times.

I was very well pleased with the sight of a fine
lady that I have often seen walk in Gray's Inn
Walks. To Madam Turner's, and dined with her.
She had heard Parson Herring take his leave ;
though he, by reading so much of the Common
Prayer as he did, hath cast himself out of the good
opinion of both sides. After dinner, to St. Dunstan's
again ; and the church quite crowded before I
come, which was just at one o'clock ; but I got
into the gallery again, but stood in a crowd. Dr.
Bates pursued his text again very well ; and only
at the conclusion told us, after this manner : ' I do
believe that many of you do expect that I should
say something to you in reference to the time,
this being the last time that possibly I may appear
here. You know it is not my manner to speak
anything in the pulpit that is extraneous to my
text and business ; yet this I shall say, that it is
not my opinion, fashion, or humour, that keeps
me from complying with what is required of us ;
but something, after much prayer, discourse, and
study, yet remains unsatisfied, and commands me
herein. Wherefore, if it is my unhappinesse not to
receive such an illuminacion as should direct me to
do otherwise, I know no reason why men should not
pardon me in this world, as I am confident that God
will pardon me for it in the next.' And so he concluded. Parson Herring read a psalme and chapters
before sermon ; and one was the chapter in the
Acts, where the story of Ananias and Sapphira is.
And after he had done, says he, ' This is just the
case of England at present. God he bids us to
preach, and men bids us not to preach ; and if
we do, we are to be imprisoned and further punished. All that I can say to it is, that I beg your

prayers, and the prayers of all good Christians, for us.' This was all the exposition he made of the chapter in these very words, and no more. I was much pleased with Bates's manner of bringing in the Lord's Prayer after his owne ; thus, ' In whose comprehensive words we sum up all our imperfect desires ; saying, " Our Father," ' &c. I hear most of the Presbyters took their leaves to-day, and that the City is much dissatisfied with it. I pray God keep peace among men in their rooms, or else all will fly a-pieces ; for bad ones will not go down with the City." [Pepys, 17th August, 1662.]

"Being the Sunday when the Common Prayer-Book, reformed and ordered to be used for the future, was appointed to be read, and the solemn League and Covenant to be abjured by all the incumbents of England under penalty of losing their livings ; our vicar read it this morning." [Evelyn, 17th August, 1662.]

At Pepys's church, St. Olave's, Hart Street, the official church of the Navy Office, the minister did not become very conversant with the new service : "Up, and I put on my best cloth black suit and my velvet cloak, and with my wife in her best laced suit to Church, where we have not been these nine or ten weeks. A young simple fellow did preach ; slept soundly all the sermon. Our parson, Mr. Mills, his own mistake in reading of the service, was very remarkable—that instead of saying, ' We beseech t!.ee to preserve to our use the kindly fruits of the earth,' he cries, ' Preserve to our use our gracious Queen Katherine ! ' " [Pepys, 17th April, 1664.]

One result of the Act was to eject from the Church of England a big Puritan element : " The

late outing of the Presbyterian clergy, by their
not renouncing the Covenant as the Act of Parliament commands, is the greatest piece of state now
in discourse. But, for ought I see, they are gone
out very peaceably, and the people not so much
concerned therein as was expected." [Pepys, 21st
September, 1662.]

Attempts to worship publicly in any other
fashion than that of the Church of England were
punished : " I saw several poor creatures carried
by, by constables, for being at a conventicle. They
go like lambs, without any resistance. I would to
God they would either conform, or be more wise,
and not be catched." [Pepys, 7th August, 1664.]

Meantime signs were not wanting of a more
enlightened policy. Pepys declared on 4th September, 1668, that the business of abusing the Puritans
begins to grow stale, and of no use, they being the
people that, at last, will be found the wisest."

The King wanted toleration, probably to benefit
the Roman Catholics : " He tells me that the King
is for Toleration, though the Bishops be against
it : and that he do not doubt but it will be carried
in Parliament ; but that he fears some will stand
for the tolerating of Papists with the rest ; and
that he knows not what to say, but rather thinks
that the sober party will be without it, rather than
have it upon those terms ; and I do believe so."
[Pepys, 31st January, 1668.]

The nation, however, feared this " plot " of the
English monarch to help the Roman Catholics,
and Evelyn is but echoing the general feeling when
on 4th April, 1672, he writes : " I went to see the
fopperies of the Papists at Somerset-House and
York-House, where now the French Ambassador

had caused to be represented our Blessed Saviour at the Pascal Supper with his Disciples, in figures and puppets made as big as the life, of wax-work, curiously clad and sitting round a large table, the room nobly hung, and shining with innumerable lamps and candles : this was exposed to all the world ; all the City came to see it. Such liberty had the Roman Catholics at this time obtained."

When James II., an avowed Roman Catholic, came to the throne, he made great efforts to give relief to his co-religionists. Louis XIV. in France was working strenuously for the Roman Catholics : " The French persecution of the Protestants raging with the utmost barbarity, exceeded even what the very heathens used : innumerable persons of the greatest birth and riches leaving all their earthly substance, and hardly escaping with their lives, dispersed through all the countries of Europe. The French tyrant abrogated the Edict of Nantes which had been made in favour of them, and without any cause ; on a sudden demolishing all their churches, banishing, imprisoning, and sending to the galleys all the ministers ; plundering the common people, and exposing them to all sorts of barbarous usage by soldiers sent to ruin and prey on them ; taking away their children ; forcing people to the Mass, and then executing them as relapsers ; they burnt their libraries, pillaged their goods, eat up their fields and substance, banished or sent the people to the galleys, and seized on their estates. There had now been numbered to pass through Geneva only (and that by stealth, for all the usual passages were strictly guarded by sea and land) 40,000 towards Switzerland. In Holland, Denmark, and all about Germany, were dispersed some hundred

thousands ; besides those in England, where,
though multitudes of all degree sought for shelter
and welcome as distressed Christians and confes-
sors, they found least encouragement, by a fatality
of the times we were fallen into, and the unchari-
table indifference of such as should have embraced
them ; and I pray it be not laid to our charge.
The famous Claude fled to Holland ; Allix and
several more came to London, and persons of great
estates came over, who had forsaken all. France
was almost dispeopled, the bankers so broken, that
the tyrant's revenue was exceedingly diminished,
manufactures ceased, and everybody there, save
the Jesuits, abhorred what was done, nor did the
Papists themselves approve it. What the further
intention is, time will show ; but doubtless por-
tending some revolution." [Evelyn, *3rd November*,
1685.]

In the next year in England James obtained a
decision from the judges which enabled him to set
at naught the acts passed against Dissenters :
" The new very young Lord Chief-Justice Herbert
declared on the bench, that the government of
England was entirely in the King ; that the Crown
was absolute ; that penal laws were powers lodged
in the Crown to enable the King to force the execution of the law, but were not bars to bind the
King's power ; that he could pardon all offences
against the law, and forgive the penalties, and why
could he not dispense with them ; by which the
Test was abolished ? Every one was astonished.
Great jealousies as to what would be the end of
these proceedings." [Evelyn, *27th June*, 1686.]

Of this he quickly made use : " Was sealed at
our office the Constitution of certain Commissioners

to take upon them full power of all Ecclesiastical affairs, in as unlimited a manner, or rather greater, than the late High Commission-Court, abrogated by Parliament ; for it had no only faculty to inspect and visit all Bishops' dioceses, but to change what laws and statutes they should think fit to alter among the Colleges, though founded by private men ; to punish, suspend, fine, &c., give oaths and call witnesses. The main drift was to suppress zealous preachers. In sum, it was the whole power of a Vicar-General—note the consequence ! Of the Clergy the Commissioners were the Archbishop of Canterbury [Sancroft], Bishop of Durham [Crewe], and Rochester [Sprat] ; of the Temporals, the Lord Treasurer, the Lord Chancellor [Jefferies] (who alone was ever to be of the quorum), the Chief Justice [Herbert], and Lord President [Earl of Sunderland]." [Evelyn, 14th July, 1686.]

James then granted freedom of worship to all —Roman Catholics as well as Protestants—by his Declarations of Indulgence : " In the last week, there was issued a Dispensation from all obligations and tests, by which Dissenters and Papists especially had public liberty of exercising their several ways of worship, without incurring the penalty of the many Laws and Acts of Parliament to the contrary. This was purely obtained by the Papists, thinking thereby to ruin the Church of England, being now the only Church which so admirably and strenuously opposed their superstition. There was a wonderful concourse of people at the Dissenters' meeting-house in this parish, and the parish-church [Deptford] left exceeding thin. What this will end in, God Almighty only knows ;

but it looks like confusion, which I pray God avert."
[Evelyn, 10th April, 1688.]

It was the order that the second Declaration must be read in all churches that brought about the opposition from the famous seven bishops : " The King enjoining the ministers to read his Declaration for giving liberty of conscience (as it was styled) in all the churches of England, this evening, six Bishops, Bath and Wells, Peterborough, Ely, Chichester, St. Asaph, and Bristol, in the name of all the rest of the Bishops, came to his Majesty to petition him, that he would not impose the reading of it to the several congregations within their dioceses ; not that they were averse to the publishing it for want of due tenderness towards Dissenters, in relation to whom they should be willing to come to such a temper as should be thought fit, when that matter might be considered and settled in Parliament and Convocation ; but that, the Declaration being founded on such a dispensing power as might at pleasure set aside all laws ecclesiastical and civil, it appeared to them illegal, as it had done to the Parliament in 1661 and 1672, and that it was a point of such consequence, that they could not so far make themselves parties to it, as the reading of it in church in time of Divine Service amounted to.

The King was so far incensed at this address, that he with threatening expressions commanded them to obey him in reading it at their perils, and so dismissed them." [Evelyn, 18th May, 1688.]

" This day the Archbishop of Canterbury, with the Bishops, Ely, Chichester, St. Asaph, Bristol, Peterborough, and Bath and Wells, were sent from the Privy Council prisoners to the Tower, for refusing to give bail for their appearance, on their not reading the Declaration for liberty of conscience ; they refused to give bail, as it would have prejudiced their Peerage. The concern of the people for them was wonderful, infinite crowds on their knees begging their blessing, and praying for them as they passed out of the barge along the Tower-wharf." [Evelyn, *8th June*, 1688.]

" Being the first day of Term, the Bishops were brought to Westminster on Habeas Corpus, when the indictment was read, and they were called on to plead ; their Counsel objected that the warrant was illegal ; but, after long debate, it was over-ruled, and they pleaded. The Court then offered to take bail for their appearance ; but this they refused, and at last were dismissed on their own recognizances to appear that day fortnight ; the Archbishop in £200, the Bishops £100 each." [Evelyn, *15th June*, 1688.]

" They appeared ; the trial lasted from nine in the morning to past six in the evening, when the Jury retired to consider of their verdict, and the Court adjourned to nine the next morning. The Jury were locked up till that time, eleven of them being for an acquittal ; but one (Arnold, a brewer) would not consent. At length he agreed with the others. The Chief Justice, Wright, behaved with great moderation and civility to the Bishops. Alibone, a Papist, was strongly against them ; but Holloway and Powell being of opinion in their favour, they were acquitted. When this was heard, there was great rejoicing ; and there was a lane of people from the King's Bench to the waterside, on their knees, as the Bishops passed and repassed, to beg their blessing. Bonfires were made that night, and bells rung, which was taken very ill at Court, and an appearance of nearly sixty Earls and Lords, &c., on the bench, did not a little comfort them ; but indeed they were all along full of comfort and cheerful.

"Note, they denied to pay the Lieutenant of the Tower (Hales, who used them very surlily) any fees, alleging that none were due." [Evelyn, *29th June*, 1688.]

On the night of the acquittal of the bishops an invitation was sent to William of Orange who came and drove James from the throne. One of the first tasks of the new monarch was to get Parliament to pass an act of toleration. Parliament now acquiesced as the Roman Catholics were not to benefit by it. Still, restricted as the act was, it was the real starting place for greater liberties in the future : "Now appeared the Act of Indulgence for the Dissenters, but not exempting them paying dues to the Church of England Clergy, or serving in office according to law, with several other clauses." [Evelyn, *26th May*, 1689.]

LONDON AND GLASGOW: COLLINS' CLEAR-TYPE PRESS.